YORKSHIRE HANGMEN

Yorkshire Hangmen

The lives and careers of hangmen born or working in Yorkshire from 1800 to the end of hanging

STEPHEN WADE

Wharncliffe Books

First Published in Great Britain in 2008 by
Wharncliffe Books
an imprint of
Pen and Sword Books Ltd
47 Church Street
Barnsley
South Yorkshire
S70 2AS

Copyright © Stephen Wade 2008

ISBN: 978-1-84563-050-8

Typeset in 11/13pt Plantin by Concept, Huddersfield.

Printed and bound in England by CPI UK

Pen and Sword Books Ltd incorporates the Imprints of
Pen & Sword Aviation, Pen & Sword Maritime,
Pen & Sword Military, Wharncliffe Books,
Pen & Sword Select, Pen and Sword Military Classics
and Leo Cooper.

For a complete list of Pen & Sword titles please contact
PEN & SWORD BOOKS LIMITED
47 Church Street
Barnsley
South Yorkshire
S70 2AS
England
E-mail: enquiries@pen-and-sword.co.uk
Website: www.pen-and-sword.co.uk

Contents

Introduction

There are many words for this profession: doomster, mate of death, staffman, the topping cove – but he is simply the 'hangman'. This was the man who had the resolve and the will to walk on a scaffold with a pinioned man, place a hood on the man's head, slip on a prepared noose so that it knotted at just the right point, perhaps whisper a final word and pull a lever that would send the victim to eternity. When James Berry, from Bradford, applied for the job, he wrote:

> I beg most respectfully to apply to you, to ask if you will permit me to conduct the execution of the two convicts now lying under sentence of death at Edinburgh. I was very intimate with Mr Marwood and he made me thoroughly acquainted with his system of carrying out his work ...

It suggests a certain quality of smooth confidence, entirely devoid of defined motivation for doing the work. It could have been a brief to build a new apartment block. Berry noted that he had seen Mr Calcraft 'execute three persons at Manchester thirteen years ago'. The magistrates of Edinburgh must have thought that they had the right kind of obsessive on their hands. For more than a decade he had harboured a wish to do what Calcraft had done, and he had been apprentice to the Lincolnshire man who had studied how to kill by asphyxiation rather than slow strangling.

Yorkshire has had no monopoly of these types, but certainly more than her fair share.

For centuries of English history, men and women were killed by judicial sanction and command, either by hanging or be-heading. In some instances there were killings more barbarous than we can imagine today, such as the fact that until the early nineteenth century we had a law on the statute books that meant a wife killing a husband would be burned to death whereas a husband killing a wife would be hanged. Until Sir

Robert Peel's first spell at the Home Office in the 1820s there were over 200 capital crimes in the criminal law known as the 'Bloody Code.' The deaths of felons on the scaffold meant a major public spectacle, something to rival a popular drama on stage or a bear-baiting contest. Crowds would turn out, some to abuse and revile a murderer and some to hope that the recreant would pray and beg for pardon, make a noble speech and call on his God.

Of course, they would not leap to their deaths and save the state a task: someone had to hang them or behead them, burn them or draw and quarter them. In most cases it was a job for the hangman. From the earliest period, these men were convicts turned executioner to save their skin or to avoid transportation. It was an occupation that existed on the cusp between ghoulish horror and grudging, awesome respect. Some hangmen were to become minor celebrities and earned money lecturing; others wrote memoirs. But on the other hand, many were ruined by drink or took their own lives. The hangman was a figure of dark and menacing myth: a character to frighten children or inhabit a Gothic mystery tale. As the nineteenth century wore on, they became the focus of much media interest, more fascinating to the Victorians as attitudes to hanging changed, moving from public to private after 1868, and always going on while agitators and reformists battled for its abolition. The work of the hangman and the spectacle of the death on the scaffold attracted many famous people: Charles Dickens had a fascination with execution and wrote against its continuance, with fervour and conviction. Thomas Hardy, whose character Tess is hanged at the end of *Tess of the D'Urbervilles,* relished the sight of criminals at the end of a rope and he wrote fiction that involved the myths and superstitions around hanging.

The hangman did a job that very few would even consider doing. Despite the fact that many of them wrote down their reasons for doing that awful duty for the state, the deep motivations in them are still perhaps a mystery. The journalist Robert Patrick Wilson, in his memoirs, writes of a meeting with William Calcraft the Essex hangman in which he is given the simplest but perhaps most tenable reason: that good citizens would all be murdered in their beds if the killers were not removed from existence. Would it were that simple; the truth is that for the century and a half covered by this book, it is certain that several people were hanged for minor thefts; women were hanged and in disgusting legal contexts of failure, insensitivity and bungling; some teenagers were hanged and also some people undoubtedly since proved innocent of the crime.

When Wilson ventured into Newgate, in 1870, he recalled a story that educates us today with regard to the sheer inhumanity of the execution process before the innovations of William Marwood who implemented a more informed method of using the knot and drop distance to make death more speedy. Wilson wrote about a hanging of a man called Jeffreys:

> When Jeffreys walked on the scaffold and reached the drop he faced St. Sepulchre's church. Calcraft hurriedly and very forcibly turned him round with his back to the church. The awful ceremony occupied a very much longer time than is now taken to bring about death. Calcraft was compelled to walk several yards along the scaffold and return the same way beneath it. All this time the wretched person remained in full view of a densely packed crowd, until with a wild shout from the mob, the condemned dropped . . .

There had been centuries of such bungling, delay and torture, as death was unnecessarily prolonged, with little thought given to the consideration of the convict's situation.

The hangmen of Yorkshire were, in the first phase of this history, mostly men working in York; this extended well into the nineteenth century when Armley Gaol came on the scene as a place with a death cell and scaffold, as a consequence of the assizes passing from York to Leeds. But York has gone down in the history books as the place where several infamous villains and also a number of political prisoners either exited the world or spent years being forgotten by the world. York was where Turpin was hanged, on the Knavesmire; it was where Askern and Curry practised their hangman's craft, the latter coping with his drink problem as he had more and more trade coming his way, particularly difficult for him when he had to hang women.

The dominating figure of James Berry from Bradford takes centre stage after that period, when he travelled the country as the national hangman. He was a complex character, and his memoirs, along with material in a recent biography of him, provide us with a profound insight into the stresses and strains of the work. He might have had a business card and seemed to revel in the notoriety his work brought, but the fact is that after he retired he was contemplating suicide and was only saved from that fate by a chance encounter with an evangelist on a railway platform.

The assistant hangmen have left little as historical record, but we have fragments about the Huddersfield man, Thomas Scott. Also Bartholomew Binns, a shopkeeper from Dewsbury, is something of a one-dimensional figure. But as soon as we move into the dynasties of hangmen we have much more in the historical record: the profession certainly ran in families up until the abolition of the death penalty in 1964: first the Billingtons and then the Pierrepoints fulfilled the role for a very long time. Steve Fielding's recent biography of the Pierrepoints has revealed details we did not have before about the remarkable Albert Pierrepoint in particular, subject of a film in 2006, to add to the public awareness of this occupation.

The last group of hangmen in the final twenty years of hanging proved to be fascinating studies of the mentalities and dispositions of people drawn to the craft. Steve Wade of Doncaster and Syd Dernley from North Nottinghamshire illustrate clearly the bizarre eccentricity of dark humour and coldness of the hangman. Dernley courted the camera and the media; Steve Wade was the opposite, a man who ran a bus company in Doncaster at one time, and then spent time helping to hang German spies at Wandsworth.

Hanging as the state's penalty for murder goes back a very long way; it was the usual method used in Anglo-Saxon times. The gallows were used by those peoples, and as one historian has written, in the Middle Ages: 'Every town, every abbey and almost every large manorial lord had the right of hanging, and a gallows or tree, with a man hanging upon it, was so frequent an object in the country, that it seems to have been considered as almost a natural an object of a landscape ...' Some of the earliest hangings in Yorkshire that we have on record are those inflicted by the Admiral of the Humber, from 1451, when the Court of Admiralty of the Humber had this written direction for justices:

> You masters of the quest, if you ... discover or disclose anything of the King's Secret counsel, or of the counsel of your fellows ... you are to be, and shall be, had down to the low water mark, where must be made three times, O Yes, for the King, and then this punishment, by the law prescribed, shall be executed upon them ...

Before the proper records of Victorian hangings were kept, it becomes harder to find statistics on the range of crimes for which men were hanged, but one record from 1835 gives some facts about Lincoln hangings and these provide a list typical of all parts of the land: the list shows the horrible difference mentioned above, between hanging for wife-murder and burning for husband murder (which was high treason, not murder, technically). The writer notes: '1722: Eleanor Elsam burnt to death near the gallows for the murder of her husband.' Then the statistics for the century after 1725 show that thirty-one hangings were for murder and most others for highway robbery or stealing of cattle. But there were executions for sodomy, rape and theft in that period.

Of course, Yorkshire also contained the infamous Halifax gibbet, so the county gained a terrible reputation regarding crime and punishment. The old lines of 'From Hull and Halifax and Hell the good Lord deliver us' certainly comes partly from that old gibbet lore. The general common law of the land, not allowing localities to execute their own criminals, had not applied to Halifax. It was useful in deterring the thieves who were likely to cut and run away with cloth on frames around the Calder valley. From 1541, forty-nine people were beheaded on the gibbet. One entry for 1623 explains a great deal about the attitudes behind this punishment: 'George Fairbank, an abandoned scoundrel, commonly called Skoggin because of his wickedness, together with Anna his spuria (pretended) daughter, both of them were deservedly beheaded on account of their manifest thefts.'

But Halifax was the exception to a general rule of law which, from early in the nineteenth century through to the final hangings in Manchester in 1964, relied on the noose as a deterrent. Whether it was such a thing or not is open to debate, but along with the story of Yorkshire's hangmen comes the ongoing fight to abolish the death penalty. Few private citizens were as zealous in that cause then Violet van der Elst, whose book, *On the Gallows*, chronicles a series of hangings and reprieves as dramatic as anything in the records themselves. She became a familiar figure around the Yorkshire prisons, and elsewhere, being noisy and obstructive in her pursuit of abolition.

More traditionally, with campaigns being done through official channels, we have a succession of reformers, from Samuel Romilly in the Regency period through to Arthur Koestler in the 1950s; their stories inevitably involved part of the records of the lives of hangmen.

In assembling these stories, I have been indebted to several people and places: the encyclopaedic writings of John Eddleston on hangings have been invaluable, together with the biographies of Berry and of the Pierrepoints by Stewart Evans and Steve Fielding. Help from Jo Jenkinson at Doncaster Metropolitan Borough Council Archives and staff at the University of Hull was very useful indeed. The expert in the history and mechanics of hanging is undoubtedly Geoffrey Abbot, whose numerous books provide all the nasty features of official death that an historian could need. Richard Clark's website is a great resource (see bibliography), as is also the material in The Black Museum publications as summarised some years ago by Gordon Honeycombe.

Material in the memoirs of judges, barristers and forensic scientists have also been useful; these records often enlighten the layman as to how and why the judiciary in past times manipulated the law courts and the developing adversarial trial to introduce compromise and adaptation when it came to choices between a 'result' of death or penal servitude. In everyday terms, in murder trials involving theft, juries and legal professionals would stealthily reduce the value of the stolen goods below the threshold value for hanging when it seemed right to do so.

Finally, thanks go to Laura Carter for the line drawings; she continues to add a powerful dimension to the narratives I try to assemble.

CHAPTER 1

The Ritual: Custom and Chaos

etween 1814 and 1834, a total of 4,731 people were sentenced to be hanged for burglary. Those who were actually executed numbered only 233. In murder charges, the ratio was 311 hanged from 359 sentenced to hang. These figures tell us a great deal about the real use and application of the ultimate punishment. The figures exclude treason and high treason and in those cases the sentences were carried out in all but a few instances. What happened in many cases was that the royal pardon was quite often exercised, with the system of the recorders' reports being gone through at meetings, sorting out those who should die for murder. Other re-prieves or pardons in that period would have been rare.

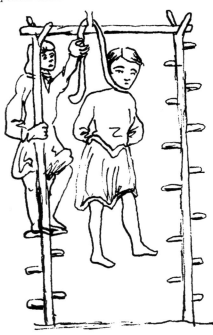

Drawing of a hanging in the Anglo Saxon period. Author's collection

In the first few decades of the period covered here, the office of Home Secretary was not the focus for pardons; Robert Peel began to change all that when he sometimes openly challenged and negated pardons given by the King. In murders, there is no doubt that most hanged and that crime and punishment give us the established media image of the hanging. The process of a murder hunt, capture and trial gradually became a major literary and cultural narrative as the popular press developed.

The drama is there in a natural structure of emotionally charged events:

1. The murder itself and circumstances around it.
2. The pursuit of the killer.
3. The arrest and imprisonment.
4. The trial.
5. The execution.
6. The moral or religious statement/penitence.

In the eighteenth century and earlier, the ordinaries (gaolers) of Newgate would take down the condemned person's biographical statements and an account of the crime in question. Then came the stories of *The Newgate Calendar*, first published in 1773 and reprinted and enlarged through to 1826, establishing the scaffold literature and the more generally understood hangman tales that gave the public its knowledge of the 'narrative of the noose'.

A typical hanging in the years before the changing attitudes of the mid-Victorian years is the execution of James Waller, who had shot and killed the gamekeeper at Hawkesworth Hall in Bingley in 1862. One report, written in 1890, is structured in the usual manner: the crime is summarised, then 'the confession of the culprit' and finally his death. If we break down the ritual of Waller's hanging, we have this sequence of events: the atmosphere and the crowd/feeling of expectancy; religious persons then distributed tracts, seeing an opportune moment to reflect on death; the Under-Sheriff then arrived to formally demand the body of Waller and he was pinioned; after that a line of dignitaries and officials stepped into place. The penultimate action was either repentance or defiance. Waller chose the former: 'Before the execution, he fell upon his knees whilst the prayers were read, and he responded to the Lord's Prayer in the most earnest manner.'

The final act was of course the culprit's submission to his fate. This is where the nature of the hangman came into play. Swiftness and humanity were called for as a general rule of course, but at that time hanging was not an exact art: 'His struggles were rather severe, but life was extinct in less than a couple of minutes.' After that, the dead man would either be

PUNISHMENT, ENGLAND.

Capital Punishment.

RULES DATED JUNE 5, 1902, MADE BY THE SECRETARY OF STATE FOR THE HOME DEPARTMENT, PURSUANT TO THE PROVISIONS OF THE CAPITAL PUNISHMENT AMENDMENT ACT, 1868,* FOR REGULATING THE EXECUTION OF CAPITAL SENTENCES.

1902. No. 444.

1. For the sake of uniformity, it is recommended that executions should take place in the week following the third Sunday after the day on which sentence is passed, on any week day but Monday, and at 8 a.m.

2. The mode of execution, and the ceremonial attending it to be the same as heretofore in use.

3. A public notice, under the hands of the sheriff and the Governor of the prison, of the date and hour appointed for the execution to be posted on the prison gate not less than twelve hours before the execution, and to remain until the inquest has been held.

4. The bell of the prison, or, if arrangements can be made for that purpose, the bell of the parish or other neighbouring church, to be tolled for 15 minutes after the execution.

5. The person or persons engaged to carry out the execution should be required to report themselves at the prison not later than 4 o'clock on the afternoon preceding the execution, and to remain in the prison from the time of their arrival until they have completed the execution, and until permission is given them to leave.

Chas. T. Ritchie,
One of His Majesty's Principal
Secretaries of State.

Whitehall,
5th June, 1902.

* 31 & 32 Vict. c. 24.

The Home Office directions for the process of capital punishment, 1902. HMSO

interred within the precincts of York Castle or, as in the case of the Leeds poisoner, Mary Bateman, the corpse was sent to an infirmary for use in dissection. The body would usually be quicklimed as well, to aid the process of decomposition.

Above and beyond that ritual sequence there were several other elements. In later times, a bell had to be sounded and sometimes there were other local indications of death. But then there was the public spectacle, and this led to the sheer chaos and barbarity of the hanging before 1868, when convicts died in the confines of prison grounds. We have a clear indication of what kinds of behaviour were common in the words used in an Act of Council dated 1737. In this edict, the authorities state that punishment awaits those who

Mary Evans, hanged at York, 1799. York Art Gallery

'throw dung and other garbage at the officers of the law, city-guard or common executioner'. They are threatened with being whipped through the city 'by the hand of the common executioner'. Here we have a detail of one of the other duties sometimes performed by the hangman. He was, in the days before Victoria's reign, someone who would administer other forms of physical punishment when needed.

The riots and violence at executions could be extremely dangerous and take place on a large scale. In many cases, the trouble was started by the actions of the reckless, abandoned types who were aggressively defiant on the scaffold, showing

An execution at Tyburn, York, 1799. Author's collection

the type of behaviour Robert Burns writes of in his song,
MacPherson's Farewell:

> Sae rantingly, sae wantonly,
> Sae dauntingly gae'd he.
> He played a tune and he danced it around
> All abone the gallows tree.

An execution at the New Drop. Author's collection

The Three-Legged Mare of York where Turpid died. Author's collection

The sheer scale of the public spectacle and excitement of a public hanging beggars belief. On the day of the hanging, any inns and hostelries near the gallows and scaffold would prepare for a massive crowd of customers, the more wealthy paying extra for the best seats in the place, those spots having a clear view of the gallows. Fights and brawls were common, and of course these occasions were potentially very profitable affairs for local tradespeople, from fruit-sellers to prostitutes.

In an article written in 1840, when hangings were still public, one journalist recalled the execution of Lord Ferrers, executed in 1760 for murdering his steward. The whole affair was a farce, with the two hangmen fighting for ownership of the rope (it could be sold for a handsome profit) and a massive crowd having a real influence on events. As the writer of 1840 noted: 'When they came to Tyburn, his coach was detained some minutes by the conflux of people.' Then, there was the pressure to make a speech and indulge in some public contrition. Ferrers was severely pressured to do this by a clergyman, who told him that 'the world will expect some satisfaction'. In other words, the condemned person was expected to be something of a star on his or her 'big day' and indulge in some rhetoric. Ferrers replied: 'Sir, what have I to do with the world?'

The crowd also stopped Ferrers' procession of officials and hangmen en route as the aristocrat had asked for a drink. The sheriff was frightened at the thought of the crowd should his charge be allowed to stop; he said: 'Your Lordship is sensible of the great influence of the crowd: we must draw up at some tavern and the conflux would be so great that it would delay the expedition which your Lordship seems to desire.' Ferrers settled for a plug of tobacco instead.

In addition to all this, there is also the material associated with the hangman's skills (or lack of them). Two York hangmen, Curry and Askern, had difficulties with drink and with the essential alacrity required in despatching their charges into death. Central to the profession was the knowledge of the knotting needed and the length of the drop. Before the more enlightened times brought on by Marwood of Horncastle in the 1870s, there was a steady realisation that established practice was barbarous. England had been hanging people since the fifth century, and in most cases the victim had to have his legs pulled by the hangmen or by waiting family members, to hasten death.

Plan of York Castle Prison. Author's collection

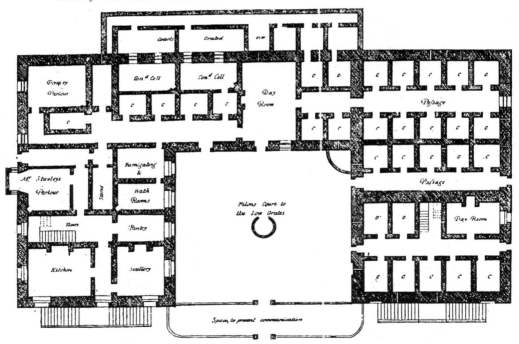

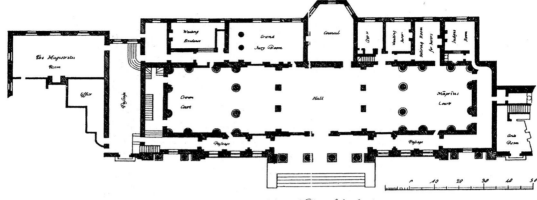

Plan of York Castle Assize Courts. Author's collection

This was because knotting was done rather casually and with no knowledge of the essential anatomy involved.

With hindsight, and with modern sensibilities, it is hard to understand why it took so long for authorities to exercise their minds with regard to the nature of body weight and length of the drop, as well as attention given to the placing of the knot. Hangmen since Marwood have all been aware of those factors: the acceleration of the fall due to gravity, bodyweight and also what the knot actually causes to happen on the vertebrae. We know now that the knot, the drop and the downward momentum cause a rupture of the spinal cord and that the actual force of impact on the falling body's neck is around 2,000 lb of force.

The placing of the knot under the left side of the jaw was also crucially important. There were several examples of things going wrong in that context. In Liverpool in 1883, Henry Dutton killed his wife's grandmother and was sentenced to hang. Yorkshireman Batholomew Binns arrived to do the job, and it turned out to be one of the worst botched executions in the records. Binns had been assistant to Marwood but had not learned well.

Dutton's final walk to his death was in line with regulations; but the drama started when Binns did the final pinioning and strapping ready for the lever to be pulled. The clock for eight had not struck and Binns walked to look at his victim, causing a

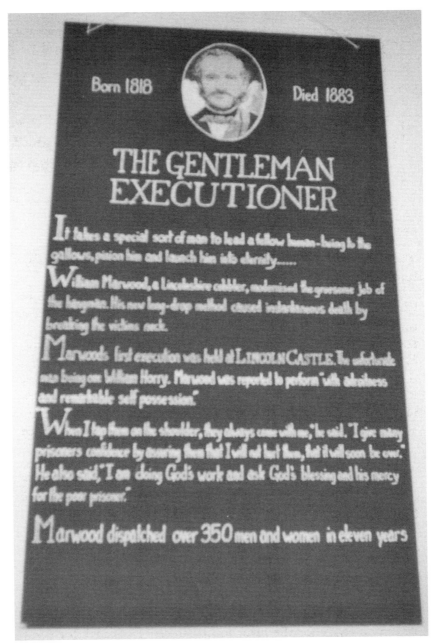

Marwood, still figuring in Lincoln Castle entertainment. Author's collection

rather nervous atmosphere. Dutton asked Lord Jesus to receive his soul, the clock struck eight and the lever was pulled. Dutton dropped but it was not a quick death. The doctor looked down at the struggling man, who was doing the 'gallows dance' and said: 'This is poor work, he is not yet dead.' In a drop of almost seven and a half feet, the body spun and the man did not die for several minutes. It was outrageously cruel by any standards. The doctor could see what the problem was: a very thick rope had been used (like a ship's hawser, the doctor said) and Dutton was very short, only five feet two inches. The result was what every hangman feared: slow strangulation rather than a snapping of the spinal column with speed.

William Marwood studied the subject of hanging for some time before taking up the official post. When he did become the hangman for the land he executed around 350 people; before taking up that post, he practised by using a trapdoor of the hoist of a warehouse on Wharf Road, Horncastle, to perfect what became known as 'the long drop.' We know about his theoretical thinking that underpinned his success with a noose, largely because he

William Marwood. Laura Carter

wrote letters to various people, including these words from a letter written in 1879, explaining his expertise (the spelling is as he wrote):

In reply to your letter ... I will give you a Compleat Staitment for executing the prisoner. 1 – Place pinion the prisoner round the Boadey and trems [tremendously] tight. 2 – Place bair the neck. 3 place – take the prisoner to the drop. 4 place – place the prisoner beneath the beam and stand direct from top of beam. 5 place – strap the prisoner's leggs tight. [sic] 6 place – putt on the cap. 7 place – put on the rope round the neck tight. 8 Let the cap be down in

John Howard, the prison reformer. Author's collection

front 9 place executioner to go direct quick to the leaver. Let down the trapdoors quick.

The customary process of hanging, handed down from sheer raw experience, was the order of the day before this. The motivations of hangmen were initially survival, as was the case with Askern of York, a man turned hangman from convict. But in earlier years, before 1800, it was not always the hangman who did the work throughout the county. Some towns would control the execution of offenders in their own way; manors and abbots could also assume that responsibility. In some places, it would be the town bailiff who would assume the hangman's role. The traditions were unnecessarily barbaric, and not only in the hanging itself. John Howard, the prisoner reformer, wrote in his classic work, *The State of the Prisons* (1777) about the related

Cobb Hall, where hangings in Lincoln took place. Author's collection

custom of 'thumbing' – another role of the hangman: 'Here I cannot forebear mentioning a practice which probably had its origins from the ancient mode of torture, though now it seems only a matter of form. When prisoners capitally charged are brought up to receive sentence ... the executioner slips a whip-cord noose about their thumbs ...'

Details such as this point to the persistence of medieval or Saxon customs in hangings, both metropolitan and provincial. The Yorkshire hangmen were to prove a particular breed, sometimes very much influenced by such customs, and often rather darkly enjoying the publicity involved in their work.

CHAPTER 2

A Short History of Capital Punishment in England Since c.1800

There has been hanging as a punishment for murder since the Anglo-Saxon period. By the end of the fifteenth century seven capital crimes were decided on: treason, petty treason, murder, robbery, larceny, rape and arson. In the Tudor period Tyburn (situated at Marble Arch) becomes a permanent execution site and in that period of the Tudor monarchs the number of hangings and beheadings was very high, well into the thousands, upper classes generally beheaded and the commoners hanged.

The most profound influence on the nature of hanging in the first part of the nineteenth century was the 'Bloody Code' developing in the fifty years after the Glorious Revolution of 1688, partly done because the propertied classes wanted to defend their possessions by raising the level of deterrence with regard to offences against property. Of course, that would include the game laws under which poaching was to provide a number of capital offences on the statutes. For instance, an Act of 1764 specified a whole group of capital offences related to linen production, covering breaking into the building, destroying linen or stealing machine tools, or even cutting linen as the material was bleaching on frames. That attitude meant that capital offences would proliferate.

As transportation became an option, the notion that the criminal underclass could be removed in large numbers by being shipped to America and then later to Van Dieman's Land became an influence on the decline of hanging in terms of the statistics. But still, into the Regency period the frequency of hangings and its attendant unpleasant social trends of disorder were still a political issue. The campaign for abolition was led

N O T E S

ON A VISIT MADE TO SOME OF

THE PRISONS

IN

Scotland

AND

The North of England,

IN COMPANY WITH

ELIZABETH FRY;

WITH SOME GENERAL OBSERVATIONS ON THE
SUBJECT OF PRISON DISCIPLINE.

By JOSEPH JOHN GURNEY.

SECOND EDITION.

LONDON:

PRINTED FOR
ARCHIBALD CONSTABLE AND CO., EDINBURGH;
LONGMAN, HURST, REES, ORME, AND BROWN,
JOHN AND ARTHUR ARCH,
AND HURST, ROBINSON, AND COMPANY, LONDON.

1819.

Elizabeth Fry's reports on prisons, 1819. Author's collection

by Sir Samuel Romilly but he was active in the period when the government feared revolution in England, repeating what had happened in France. The suppression of radical activities and dissent in the press and periodicals meant that a level of paranoia in the authorities led to a belief that hanging political activists and social dissenters would solve all the ills. When the fight for the vote meant Chartism flowered, and also the Luddites were active in fighting the mechanisation of the clothing industry, there was fear in the streets. Until the 1830s there was no police force so the militia were called out to suppress such radical activities. Hangings occurred at certain times in that thirty years between c.1800–1830 sometimes in 'blanket' fashion, as with a whole tranche of executions after the Luddite attacks on mills in the West Riding. The scaffold at York Castle was often in use in those years.

Master Serjeant Talfourd, a writer on capital punishment abolition c.1820. Author's collection

Van Dieman's Land. The author

The turning point came with Sir Robert Peel stepping into the role of Home Secretary in 1822. After that, Peel set about reforming most of the principal features of the criminal justice system. That would begin to affect the nature of potential reprieves. A statistic that indicates what was changing is the fact that of sixty-two people sentenced to hang between 1827 and 1830, seven were reprieved by the Secretary of State. What happened was that at the end of each month of Old Bailey work, a ceremony known as Recorder's Report took place. The Recorder of the court would go through the list of capital offenders and ask the king to decide who should actually be hanged and who reprieved. The great Lord Eldon, who attended these for a long period, commented in his memoirs: 'We were called upon to decide on sentences, affecting no less than the lives of men, and yet there was nothing put before us that would enable us to judge whether there had been any extenuating circumstances . . .'

But in most cases, when reprieves never even came into the picture, the practice was for the judge to place the black cap on his head at the assizes and pass the death sentence. The normal practice in the years before the Victorian era was to sentence on Friday and then for the hanging to take place the next Monday. Later, a week would be added to allow a short period of time for reflection and repentance, so there would be a little more time for actions towards reprieves or further investigation.

A typical cell for those awaiting punishment, c.1830. The author

The number of capital crimes was gradually reduced after 1810. By 1861 there were only four capital crimes left. The Criminal Law Consolidation Act made, in most practical applications, only murder left as a crime with hanging attached at punishment. After that, the other main issue was about alternatives to hanging; for decades there had been the option

A penitentiary building, Port Arthur. The author

of transportation, but after 1853 the role of prison changed and the notion of penal servitude was properly established. The remaining issues in debate concerned the sensitive and difficult subjects of acceptable defences such as provocation, insanity and diminished responsibility. The topics of hanging women and young adults was also very much up for discussion and contention. By 1908 the minimum age for hanging was raised to sixteen. Only after a celebrated case in Lincolnshire in 1931 in which a fifteen-year-old shot and killed his uncle and aunt did the age threshold change again, raised to eighteen in 1933.

The courts of criminal appeal came into being in 1907 and so the high drama of the appeal being one step away from either life or death was added to the chronicle of hangings in England. At the core of this was the notion of insanity. The McNaghten Rules had governed most cases and attitudes since 1843 when Daniel McNaghten murdered the private secretary of Sir Robert Peel, Edward Drummond. The killer was suffering from delusions and was acquitted on the grounds of partial insanity. Between then and 1957 there was constant debate as to what constituted insanity, and therefore about what would save a person from the gallows. In 1957 the Homicide Act described and defined what the law saw as diminished responsibility.

The hanging of women was extremely contentious. A first step in changing legislation to allow for more understanding of the medico-legal aspects of some homicides was the Infanticide Act of 1922 which separated infanticide from murder: infanticide became a version of manslaughter.

The 1948 Universal Declaration of Human Rights was a large factor in bringing about changes of attitude. Ruth Ellis, the last woman to be hanged in England, died in 1955 and in 1964 the last two people were hanged: on 13 August that year two men were hanged: Peter Allen and Gwynne Evans in Liverpool and Manchester respectively.

In that long struggle to move away from the atrocities of judicial execution, one of the most telling episodes was the campaign to stop the burning of women for the murder of their husbands. In the House of Commons, in May 1790, Sir Benjamin Hammet spoke on the subject. The parliamentary papers for that time reported on this:

> He stated that it having been his official duty to attend on the melancholy occasion of seeing the dreadful sentence put in execution, he then designed to move for leave to bring in a bill for alteration ... The judgement of being burned alive, applied to women for certain crimes, was the savage remains of Norman policy ...

The last seven words say it all: for 700 years there had been no change; just three years before he spoke, a woman had been burned in York for husband-murder. Hammet said that several judges had urged him to press for reform. The report ends simply with the words, 'The motion was agreed to.' That particular crime of petty treason was converted to murder in 1829, though in practice most cases had not resulted in burning, but hanging, as judges took a humanitarian stance.

The courtyard gallows at York. Author's collection

As all these developments took place, there were still the hangmen, doing their dark trade, both reviled and yet often secretly admired. Why did they do it? Research suggests that motivations were not monetary ones. The hangman needed another income. John Ellis was a barber and Steve Wade ran a coach company. Some did it as they saw the work as an arm of God's retribution for sin; others as a vital part of the Mosaic law of justice: an eye for an eye. In spite of such classical texts as George Orwell's powerful essay, *A Hanging* (1931) and the various books and articles from the pens of Arthur Koestler and Fenton Bresler (see bibliography) the abolition was a very long time coming. Since 1964 several hanged people have been pardoned after work by the Criminal Cases Review Commission. What more profound and ironical defence of abolition could there be?

Within that larger picture, the present volume sets out to trace the careers and major cases of the Yorkshire hangmen, but I have also added a selection of the most intriguing and dramatic hangings taking place in Yorkshire (mainly Armley and Hull) in the prescribed period.

Part One

Hangmen Employed in Yorkshire

Curry	York
Askern	York
Howard	York
Coates	York (born in Leeds)
Binns	Dewsbury (born in Gateshead)
The Billingtons	Bolton, but working in Yorkshire
Berry	Bradford
Scott	Huddersfield
The Pierrepoints	Clayton, Bradford
Wade	Doncaster

CHAPTER 3

Curry and other York Hangmen
1800s–1870s

A year later, he was still in York Castle, presumably waiting to be sent to Australia ... when the post of hangman became vacant. (James Bland)

In the early nineteenth century York Castle prison was still the real punishment prison for Yorkshire. A report of 1820 states that Leeds prison was 'a gaol for safe custody only' and in contrast, Wakefield House of Correction for maintenance and support. In Leeds people were confined only until they could conveniently be taken before a magistrate. When convicts were convicted at Leeds sessions, they were sent to Wakefield or to York.

York had been the central prison for a long time, stretching back to the late seventeenth century when a prison was built inside the bailey. By 1783 there was also a courthouse and a female prison, to add to the debtor's prison. In terms of executions carried out at York, from the end of the fourteenth century to 1800 hangings were done on the Knavesmire, where Dick Turpin was hanged for instance, an area that is a part of the racecourse. The execution frame was based on the 'triple tree' at Tyburn in London and so it became known as the York Tyburn. This was a frame with three beams and three upright supports. Condemned people were taken there from the gaol in a cart and met their end on what became known as the 'three-legged mare'.

The hanging of Dick Turpin in 1739 was entirely typical of the tradition of having the hangman a convict turned execu-

The Old Cock Inn, *Halifax, where the 'king of the coiners' was arrested – a pre-1800 hangman's client.* Author's collection

tioner; he was hanged by Thomas Hadfield who had been sentenced to death for highway robbery. When the 'new drop' began to be used it was within the castle. Some men were hanged for sheep stealing in 1800. The place of that new drop was near Castle Mills Bridge and the river. From the arrival of that new drop, York was to have a series of hangmen, all convicts turned executioner, beginning with William Curry in 1802.

Curry was known as 'Mutton Curry' as he had two convictions for sheep stealing. Fate had been on his side, because his death sentence had been commuted twice. He was waiting to be sent to Australia on the second occasion, when he turned hangman. In fact, he was still a convicted felon, and was a prisoner as well as a hangman until 1814. Curry was to become a true local character – a man with a drink problem, and that comes as no surprise when we reflect on the nature of his work. There had been no professional training of course. A man who had turned executioner had no means of practising his trade. He could only learn by doing. The stress that came along with that was exhibited on the scaffold many times.

There is some confusion about his real identity and name; sometimes he is called John Curry but he was known as William Wilkinson as well. His date of birth was around 1761 but that is not certain. He was from Romanby and his thefts had led him deep into trouble, first in 1793 when he stole some sheep from an innkeeper at Northallerton, William Smith. He was also fortunate at that stage, in the sense that his commutation to transportation did not happen; he was sent to the Woolwich hulks. That was obviously far from pleasant, but at least he was not on his way to Van Dieman's Land. Nevertheless, Curry in his time on the prison ships would have had a very hard time; in the first thirty years in which these hulks were used, one in four convicts died. He would have spent much of his time lifting timber on the Thames shore and when he was not working he may well have suffered the fate of one young prisoner who told an enquiry that he had been in irons while working and sleeping and that he had worn the same

The Halifax gibbet – an alternative to the noose. Laura Carter

clothes for two years. He had also been flogged, and one of the worst cases of this was of an old man who had been flogged with a cat o' nine tails thirty-six times for being five minutes late for a roll-call.

But Curry came through all this, to find himself the hangman at York. His arrival at York was reported by the *York Courant* in August, 1800:

> Last week was committed to the Castle William Currey, otherwise Wilkinson, charged upon oath with stealing an ewe sheep, the property of Thomas Severs ... The above person was convicted at this castle in March 1793 ...

Curry was to be hangman there for over thirty years and hanged a very large number of people, including fourteen people all executed in one day in 1813. The tendency to fortify himself with strong drink was so notable that the local newspaper made much of that when Curry retired in 1835, writing:

> ... it is to be much regretted that, whilst preparing the final noose for his unfortunate victims, gin was apt to provide a snare for him, and that he could never be induced to adjust a hempen cord without an undue allowance of blue thread.

Arguably his most scandalous and unprofessional day's work was on 14 April 1821 when he had to hang two felons, but at separate locations. In the late morning he hanged a man in the York Castle, and then he had his appointment with Brown around 1.00 in the afternoon, and that was in the city gaol, at Baile Hill. Curry walked to the second appointment and he was recognised. Consequently he was reviled and abused; one report noted that the crowd 'hustled and insulted the executioner to such a degree during the whole of his walk that he arrived nearly exhausted, and with nerves quite inadequate to the task he still had to perform.' Curry had only one recourse: to take some drink and settle his nerves. The result was a black farce of the worst kind, at the scaffold.

What happened was that Curry was a lively, bumptious character when drunk and he realised that this was a good opportunity to play the fool a little. His black comedy led to his raising the rope with a malevolent smile and shouting at the crowd:

A multiple hanging at York. Laura Carter

'Some of you come up and I'll try it!' Things deteriorated after that. He could not do the basic things involved in the ritual of the death. The newspaper report states that: 'The executioner, in a bungling manner and with great difficulty placed the cap over the culprit's face and attempted several times to place the rope around his neck, but was unable.'

The mob were understandably restless and screamed at the sheriff to sort things out and find a man who could to the work expeditiously. But the sheriff held firm and it was only because the governor stepped forward and insisted on silence and respect that things progressed. Two other attendants helped Curry and the task was done. But Curry was the object of deep hatred and enmity. The mob screamed that he should be hanged, yelling: 'Hang Jack Ketch – he's drunk.' *The Yorkshire Gazette* reported that Curry was beaten up later when he went home.

But worse was to come in Curry's sad career of incompetence. Drink and nerves got the better of him when he had to hang five men. It happened later in 1821 and there could not be a better incident if one wanted to explain Curry's inefficiency. Clearly, hanging five men simultaneously presented logistical problems, notably in terms of the bolts and levers. With five to hang, it depended on the one bolt, and after saying their prayers, the five men were pinioned and placed in the right spots to drop into eternity. The trouble was that Curry fell with them. He had stood in the wrong place and when the bolt was swung, down he went. The crowd saw all this, of course, and the local paper reported:

Mr Triffitt, Governor of York Prison, c.1890. Laura Carter

> As soon as the drop fell a man was seen to fall upon the ground, when there was a cry of 'Oh the rope has broken' but in a minute the fear was removed, and a shout of joy burst from the crowd on observing the man get up.

It was Curry, and the crowd revelled in abusing and laughing at his plight.

It is amazing that Curry kept his job after that. But he carried on, retiring in 1835 and lived for five years in Thirsk parish workhouse. The local burial register says simply, 'William Curry of Thirsk, aged 76.' But as James Bland has pointed out, there is some doubt in this. Bland notes that there is an age discrepancy, as a calendar of felons printed in 1801 states that he was then thirty-one; that would make Curry seventy-one in 1841. But all in all, it seems as though the Curry dying in the workhouse was the hangman.

On 30 November 1839, *The York Courant* reported that there had been a daring escape from York Castle by a group of prisoners. The account says: They were James Coates, William Marshall and William Sellers ... On Wednesday evening the cells were all left apparently safe but early next morning it was found that the prisoners had in some manner at present not known escaped from them and scaled the outer walls by means of rope ladders made from bed rugs ... Coates is said to be a great adept at opening locks.

As previous research has shown, between 1824 and 1853 fifty-nine people escaped from the Castle, and Coates was the only one never recaptured. Coates was a Leeds man, and he took over from Curry but carried out just two hangings (he was still a prisoner) before the escape of 1839.

There was some difficulty on finding an immediate replacement for Curry, as is shown in the instance of Coates hanging the Sheffield man, Charles Batty. York had employed a man from Bradford, but he never came, and so Coates was persuaded to take the job. It meant that he avoided the transportation to which he had been sentenced in 1835. When he escaped, his replacement was Nathaniel Howard, a man who was not a convict. He was a coal-porter and he was sixty when he took over as hangman for Yorkshire. He was in office between 1840 and 1853 and accounts of him suggest that he found the work depressing and emotionally wearing; one report notes that after his first hanging, Howard 'appeared much affected both before and after the performance of his task'. There were eleven hangings recorded at York in that period.

Howard definitely had professional difficulties in the practice of his trade, though he managed to carry out a triple hanging in 1841 and a double hanging in 1842. But in 1853 he had the task of hanging William Dobson, a man who had killed a young girl, Catherine Sheardon, in Wakefield. The execution was a disaster from the start; Dobson was slowly strangled, dangling on the rope, and Howard apparently did not pull on the victim's legs to hasten death. It was a repulsively barbaric sight for the onlookers and it led to the man's dismissal. There was a crowd of 5,000 to witness this terrible slow death. Howard was seventy-three at the time and perhaps should not have been doing the work at all. The *York Courant* reported that the business had been 'a painful exhibition' and it showed that 'from old age and infirmity he [Howard] was incapable to perform the duties of his responsible situation'. At that time, long before William Marwood developed the long drop and worked out his 'table of drops', together with the knowledge of where to tie the knot and what rope to use, the usual practice was to strangle the victim, and for relatives of officials to pull on the legs of the hapless criminal who was being slowly strangled.

Finally, Thomas Askern appeared on the scene in 1856; he was a former prisoner, but in gaol for debt rather than for any violent offence. There must have been the usual deal done for his release a little time after taking up the post, because he was living in Rotherham in 1859. Once again, we have a man whose work is marred by bungling and incompetence. He was man with a varied career to date: farmer, butcher, flour-seller and parish overseer from Maltby. In his time in the debtors' prison he was described as 'a man without money and without friends'.

His first victim was the celebrated William Dove, who had poisoned his wife in Leeds, after a shady involvement with the 'wise man' and quack Harrison. But, as research by Owen Davies has made clear, there are some doubts about this. Askern denied that he hanged Dove and a minor controversy ensued. Dove was hanged at York on 9 August 1856 in front of a huge crowd of almost 20,000 people. He wrote to Yorkshire newspapers threatening libel if they did not withdraw their statements that he had hanged Dove. There was even a letter published in Manchester supposedly from a schoolmaster in York, saying that Askern was not the executioner of Dove. But when traced, the man denied writing that. It seems that Askern's earlier life and his debt, were indicative of a personality capable of self-deception as well as attempts at deception of others. But some inmates of the debtors' prison wrote to the *Leeds Mercury* to confirm that the man in question was indeed Askern. The hangman had actually attacked one man in the gaol with a stick for saying that he (Askern) hanged Dove.

In many of his hangings, there were errors and incompetence. In a double hanging at Armley a black cloth was put around the victims but still, despite the fact that bodies were out of sight of the crowd, a reporter said that one of the men died quickly but the other was slowly strangled over several minutes. In 1865, when he was to hang Matthew Atkinson, the rope snapped and

The asylum, Port Arthur. The author

the man fell fifteen feet; he was unhurt and stood there for
twenty minutes until Askern had a second attempt.

Arguably the most shameful bungling of Askern's career was
the case of thirty-seven-year-old John Johnson from Bradford.
On Boxing Day 1876, Johnson was enjoying a drink with
Amelia Walker at the *Bedford Arms* in Wakefield Road; everything was relaxed at first, but Amelia had other men-friends
and one of these, Amos White, came into the bar. White made
advances to her and she called for Johnson who was at the bar;
there was a fight and White was coming off best, but then
Johnson ran out, only to return shortly afterwards with a gun.
He fired the shotgun at White's chest and then bystanders
wrestled Johnson to the ground. Johnson was charged with
murder and after trial at York Assizes he was sentenced to die.
Waiting for him was Askern.

When Johnson was made ready for the last seconds, standing on the trap, on 3 April 1877, the lever was pulled but the trap broke and Johnson fell through the hole, his feet not kicking air but still on wood. He had to be sat down, groaning on a chair, attended by the gaol warders, who were always ready to help a poor criminal if the death was being handled too slowly and clumsily. Johnson had to be taken to the trapdoor and prepared again. The man's heart must have been bursting from his chest, and whatever resolve he had previously gathered was surely gone, as he tried to prepare for death a second time. It was a total outrage: the drop was only partially successful and his death was slow and horrific. He struggled for several minutes in his death throes.

According to one anonymous journalist, writing in the 1870s, Askern became a man 'shunned and despised and often liable to insults and desperate encounters in public company'. Askern had a final year in office but hanged no-one: for the one execution that did take place in that year, Marwood was brought in from Lincolnshire. Askern died in Maltby, at the age of sixty-two in 1878. After his death, the hangmen of England would be national, with general responsibilities, rather than provincial. The next Yorkshire hangmen would operate anywhere, even as far as Ireland, when needed.

After 1868 executions ceased to be public, so the barbaric days at York, described by historian G Benson were a thing of the past. Benson wrote: 'York hangings drew crowds from far and near. At such times all the roads to York were thronged. After the railway was opened many came by train and on one occasion in 1856 ... it was lamented that no cheap excursions were run.'

CHAPTER 4

Bartholomew Binns
1880s

Twenty guineas, annually paid out of the city's cash to Binns should be withdrawn. (*The Times*)

On 6 May, 1882 a teenager called James Murphy, of Thomas Street, Dublin, was walking in Phoenix Park in that city. He told a barrister later that he was alone there a little after 7.00 in the evening and then he saw a strange sight. Here are his own words:

> I was coming by the sunk trench in front of the Viceregal Lodge ... I was proceeding towards the gate in the direction of the town ... I saw a group of persons there who drew my attention. I thought they were wrestling when I perceived them at first ... When I came up on the road I saw one body lying on the road and the other on the footway. The one on the roadway first fell ... I think the car man wore a slouched hat ...

What the young man's vague description relates to is one of the formative events in Irish history: the murder of Lord Frederick Cavendish, Chief Secretary for Ireland, and his under-secretary, Mr Thomas Burke. The men who had attacked and killed them were brutal in the extreme, as the coroner said: 'The sight of the dead bodies was sufficiently shocking ... they seem to have been attacked in front, and they seem to have been unarmed and defenceless, within sight of the habituees of the park ...'

The killings were also to make the most significant experience in the life of Dewsbury executioner, Bartholomew Binns, because subsequently, an informer against the killers, the Irish

Bartholomew Binns. Laura Carter

'Invincibles' as they were known, had been shot and killed in a ship off South Africa. It became Binns' task to hang the gunman.

Binns was a Gateshead man who moved to Dewsbury where he kept a shop. He followed Marwood, the man who had revolutionised the trade of hangman in the 1870s, but he was not to be in office very long, being lead hangman rather than assistant for just a year. The reason for that was that he managed to provide a service which was an uneasy mix of smooth professional work and disastrous botched jobs. He must have had qualities that appealed to the selection board however, as he was one of a large number of applicants. His bungled execution of Dutton at Liverpool has already been described (see the introduction). But it was not only in his professional work that he attracted trouble and disagreement. In January 1884 he was on the wrong side of law himself, appearing in court for travelling without a ticket, on a trip between Huddersfield and Dewsbury. As he and his assistant, Alfred Archer, sat in the refreshment room, they were asked to produce a ticket and could not do so. Binns made an excuse, explaining that his notoriety had attracted attention and caused delays.

But it was with the hanging of Patrick O'Donnell, the killer of the 'grass' from the Phoenix Park business, that Binns reached celebrity for a short time. To his credit, his hanging of O'Donnell went well. The report in *The Times* for 18 December 1883, has this account of Binns' participation:

> Between a quarter of an hour and ten minutes before the time appointed for the execution, the bell of St Sepulcre's commenced tolling ... Immediately afterwards the civic officials, accompanied by Captain Sutton Kirkpatrick, the Governor of Clerkenwell and Newgate, and the Rev Mr Duffield ... proceeded to the condemned cell where

TERRIBLE TRAGEDY.

THE CHIEF SECRETARY
AND
UNDER SECRETARY
MURDERED.

LATEST DETAILS.

HORROR AND INDIGNATION IN THE CITY.

OPENING OF THE INQUEST.

On Saturday evening a wild and fearful rumour spread through the city, to the effect that the Chief Secretary and Under Secretary had been attacked and murdered. So startling was the statement that it was at first received generally with utter incredulity. A variety of accounts were given of the transaction. Some said the new Chief Secretary and the Under Secretary had been assailed and injured, but not killed outright; others that they had been shot dead. The truth, however, was soon discovered by inquiry at the various centres of information, and it was found that the two officials had been brutally murdered in a most cold-blooded and horrible manner. Public curiosity and interest became so intense that the newspaper offices were literally besieged, and a midnight edition of the "Evening Telegraph" was published, and when the absolute and appalling facts became known the utmost horror and indignation was felt and expressed amongst all classes of the community. The following are briefly the main outlines of the tragic event :—The Chief Secretary and the Under Secretary had been walking together in the Phœnix Park shortly after seven o'clock, when suddenly they were attacked by four men, armed with daggers or long sharp knives. The conflict, if such it may be called, must have been a brief, sharp, and decisive one, for the two unfortunate gentlemen were unarmed, and they must have been very quickly despatched.

The first brief facts ascertained of the dreadful tragedy showed that Mr. Maguire, of Amiens street, and a friend, who were riding on a tricycle, found the bodies in the place mentioned. A boy, named Jacob, states that, while birdnesting in the Park, he saw about 200 yards from where he was, and convenient to the road, a group of men as if wrestling. He thought they were roughs and did not pay much attention to them. He then saw two men fall to the ground, and four others jump on a car and drive off towards Chapelizod, which lies in the direction opposite to the city. They drove at a rapid pace, and he could not give any description of the appearance of the men.

Lord Frederick Cavendish only arrived in Dublin at noon on Saturday to take up his new office. He drove through the city in the Viceregal procession on the occasion of the State entry of his Excellency Earl Spencer. The double murder took place under circumstances which enhance its shocking character. The assassins were four in number, and the assassination took place about ten minutes past seven o'clock, quite close to the Viceregal grounds. The evening was beautifully fine, and there was, as usual, a vast number of people in the Park. A polo match, which had been carried on in the Park, had just closed a quarter of an hour before. So rapidly was the deed perpetrated, and with such instant effect that no one's attention was directed to the occurrence in any unusual degree. Even those who did observe the presence of six men imagined it was a friendly wrestling match on the part of roughs, and paid no attention to it. It appears that Lord Frederick Cavendish, after taking part in the ceremony of the installation of the Lord Lieutenant, and having been himself sworn in as Chief Secretary, proceeded on foot through the city, and through the Park, to walk to the Chief Secretary's Lodge, which is situated near the farther end of the Park, and to the left of the main road, the Viceregal Lodge being to the right, and about half a mile nearer the city. Lord

The Phoenix Park Murders: report from the Freeman's Journal. Author's collection

Bartholomew Binns, the public executioner, who had arrived at Newgate Friday evening, quickly went through the process of pinioning the convict's arms in the ordinary manner ... the executioner then secured the pinioning straps around his legs and having adjusted the ropes around the culprit's neck ... then touching a lever, the body of the unhappy man disappeared from sight.

The reporter was profoundly impressed by Binns' skill, noting that the death had been so instantaneous because, in the surgeon's opinion, there could not even have been 'a twitching of the hands'.

This all counterbalanced the Dutton fiasco in Liverpool, but it certainly made Binns well known. There is a story that, before the hanging of O'Donnell, a traveller came into Binns' shop and tried to sell song sheets about the imminent death of the 'Invincible' Fenian. When Binns did not buy one, the man went away, only to return in an aggressive mood with threats of shooting Binns. Help was summoned and the man eventually served a prison term.

But the downward spiral in his career, when it came, was speedy. First London removed him from the scene: an announcement in March 1884 stated that 'Alderman Sir Andrew Lusk MP called the attention of the court to the subject of the appointment of Bartholomew Binns to the office of hangman, and in view of what had recently taken place with reference to him, moved that the twenty guineas honorarium paid to him annually should be withdrawn.' It was withdrawn; what had happened just before that sacking was that, after another bungled hanging in Liverpool (of Mclean) he was relieved of duties in the north. He had arrived at Walton drunk and had had to be helped by a man called Samuel Heath, to complete the job.

The petty troubles and squabbles that filled Binns' life continued to the end; there was a nasty side to him, as he not only took his mother-in-law to court over alleged theft, but also, so the story went at the time, he tended to hang cats and dogs for some kind of horrible pleasure. Apparently his mother-in-law reported him for that. His final years were pathetically miserable and he even tried to earn a few pounds at fairs and feasts, explaining execution methods.

CHAPTER 5

James Berry
(in office 1884–92)

The poor creatures who were slumbering their hours away, in the prison cell just beyond where I was laid, thinking of the dreadful fate that awaited them ... (Berry's Memoir)

J ames Berry was a man who came to his vocation as hangman after a long list of failures and dead-ends in his search for a career which would satisfy him. After a rough and eventful childhood in which he narrowly escaped death or serious injury on a number of occasions, he began to take note of the work being done by Marwood in his fairly short but important reign as public executioner. Marwood, as already briefly mentioned, laboured hard to refine the art of hanging, with attention paid in more detail to the weight of the body and the length of the drop down the trapdoor. The process generally demanded a swiftly handled sequence of actions following the movements of putting on the cap, placing the noose, removing the pin in the lever-frame, pilling the lever and finally making sure the trap and drop worked.

Berry, as he noted in his letter of application after Marwood's death, made a point of stressing that he had actually met and taken advice from the Lincolnshire shoemaker. Marwood had become infamous: the rhyme, 'If pa killed ma, who would kill pa? Marwood' was in common currency and he had been immortalised at Madame Tussaud's waxworks. Berry had paid attention to the skills involved in the work, and it seems that although money was not the major consideration, it was very important to him at the time because he had a wife and family to

Lincoln Castle. The author

house and feed. Berry had served in the Bradford police and so had some knowledge of the criminal world and of the nature of urban crime, violent or otherwise. But he soon realised how different and of course, how unique the craft of executing felons actually was in practice.

It was Binns' failure that opened up the work to him; he had been pipped at the post when Binns was first employed, being second in a very long list of applicants. In fact, one of Berry's abiding faults was a bold egoism and lust for publicity as well as respect, and that very nearly cost him the career he sought. He told the press that he had the post before it was really secured.

But it appears that the selection panel were so impressed with his profile and past initiative, as well as in his long-standing interest in the work, that they appointed him gladly.

Of course, any of the figures in authority would have soon been aware, had they looked back on the previous hangmen in the century, that there was a likelihood of embarrassment and shame attached to the post, largely as a result of the tendency for the incumbents of the profession to take to drink and to suffer from what we would now call work-related stress. But something about Berry's manner and air of confidence brought him into favour.

James Berry was born in February 1852 in Heckmondwike, where his father, Daniel, was a wool-stapler. He had a hard time at school and his nature contained a strong streak of rebellion which led him to try to run away to sea, play truant and get into all kinds of scrapes. But his police service apparently caused a significant change in him, primarily in his self-regard and confidence. He wrote in his memoirs with an arrogance and vanity about his successes there (and later in the Nottingham police for a short while) with outstanding claims. His achievements read like a Sherlock Holmes of Yorkshire. But both in Bradford and in Nottingham he was restless and demanding, and his personality was abrasive and combative, leading ultimately to resignation.

He had been considering the appeal of the welcome income of the hangman's trade for some time; his range of employment had brought continual frustration and some real financial hardship. But certainly in the case of execution work, he had taken it seriously for some time. When his memoirs were first published, serialised in the *Saturday Post* magazine in 1914, he explained the source of his aims to work as hangman in this way, after he heard newsboys shouting out the news that Marwood had died:

> It almost seemed as if fate had kept me poor to drive me into the position. It seemed that I was predestined from birth to become the follower of Marwood, for, extraordinary though it may seem, the Chief Constable of Bradford was setting out to ask me to take the job at the very moment I

was setting out to ask him to use his influence with the people of London.

We have to speculate what character traits in Berry had impressed themselves on the Chief Constable, James Withers. It is very difficult to ascertain exactly what qualities would lead someone to see the potential of 'public hangman' in a person. A profile, taking in the men who have filled that role in British history, would have to include features including religious calling, odd altruistic need to participate in mosaic justice, and of course, the appeal of cash or freedom in the tradition of felons turned executioners, particularly in Yorkshire. In Berry's case, financial reward was part of it, but the superiors in the police force and perhaps also Marwood (they did meet) saw something else.

Arguably the best way to locate this elusive quality is to observe how he acquired his professionalism and that is closely recorded in the events around his very first job, in Edinburgh, in March 1884. We would expect a man to recall such an experience in great detail, and such was the case. The victims in question were two poachers, William Innes and Robert Vickers. There was still a common feeling around that poaching was a social crime, and that gamekeepers were very much reproached for their work. Some thought that the two men would have a reprieve. But it was not to be, and the account of Berry's weekend there, as retold by Stewart Evans in his recent biography of Berry, makes it clear that the Bradford man was extremely impressive, and as one would expect, he had to go through the hellish torment of that first ordeal, knowing he was taking two young lives, judicially sanctioned or not, still a kind of homicide.

Berry, with his mysterious assistant with a pseudonym of 'Richard Chester', gives an account of the whole period, from arrival on the Thursday to departure after the job was done. He certainly did his homework, doing all kinds of tests on the gallows such as using bags of cement as the body-weights and of course, calculating the drop required. His religious faith played a part, as he asked for guidance from the Almighty, but also the professionalism in him came through, seen clearly in the way

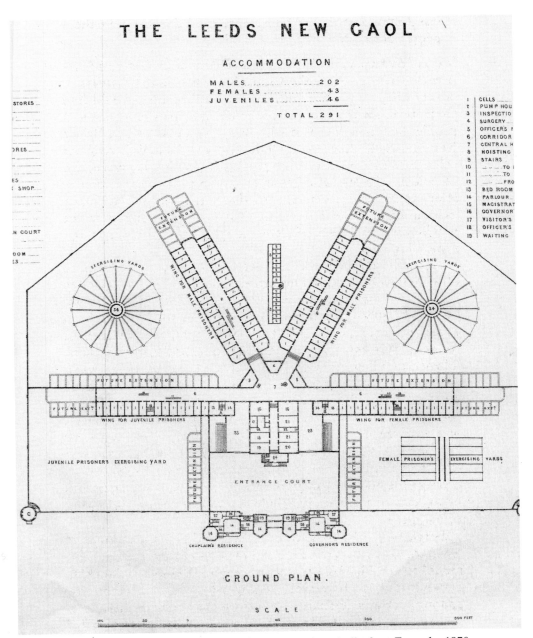

A plan of Armley Gaol. Note the strict segregation of offenders. From the 1870 report. Author's collection

his mental strength held strong against all the emotional and sympathetic thoughts that assailed him as he had to spend many long hours inside the grounds, thinking of the enormity of what he was about to do.

As Stewart Evans describes, the hanging itself was notably efficient and it pleased the officials from the prison and other medical men – a rare achievement in this trade. Berry wrote: 'Everything was done as quick as lightning, and both culprits paid the highest penalty of the law . . .' As Evans also points out (and this is a real mystery) Berry departed from Marwood's practice in one very significant way, and that was in respect of where the knot was placed on the neck. Marwood's belief, later supported by a group of surgeons, was that the knot should be fastened submentally, that is, under the chin and on the left. Berry made his knot under the left ear. That would almost certainly not be as rapid and efficient as a knot over the major artery under the left front of the chin; it would make more of a forceful jolt, affecting the spinal column differently also.

Berry only did one hanging in Yorkshire, but it was a sensational case: that of the Barnsley murderer (again, a poacher) James Murphy. He was a Dodworth collier who had experienced the urgings of a personal vendetta against a constable called Austwick. Ever since Austwick had arrested him for drunkenness, Murphy had had a burning hatred against the officer. He later went out, with a clear intention of killing Austwick and did so, then after a few days on the run he was tracked down and arrested.

Surely the most remarkable aspect of the Murphy case was his nonchalance and fortitude in the face of the scaffold. Berry has left a detailed account of the conversation he had with the killer. On entering the cell as Murphy was chewing a mutton chop, fully aware that his death was only a few hours away. At the end of the talk, Murphy made a joke. Berry asked: 'I hope you won't give me any trouble when the time comes,' and this followed:

He looked at me and smiled.

'I won't give you any trouble. I am not afraid to die. A lot of people have been making a fuss over this business, and

Armley Gaol. Laura Carter

I'm hanged if I can see what there is to make a fuss about.'

I was so surprised at his joke, that I could say nothing, and so I left him and did not see him again until I went to pinion him.

In Berry's career as hangman, he had the especially painful duty of executing five women. One of these, the case of Mary Lefley in Lincolnshire, provides one of the most heart-rending and contentious hangings in the entire record of British capital punishment. In the Lincolnshire village of Wrangle, Mary Lefley, aged forty-nine, lived with her cottager husband, William, ten years her senior. They were living in a freehold property and seemed reasonably happy as far as anyone was aware. On 6 February 1884 various friends called at their cottage and everything seemed normal. Mary set off for Boston to sell produce, and later in the day, around 3.00 in the afternoon, William arrived at the home of the local medical man, Dr Bubb. Lefley was extremely ill and the doctor was not there. He staggered in and hit the floor, retching and moaning. He had brought a bowl of rice pudding and told some women present that it had poisoned food in it.

When he was told again that Dr Bubb was not at home, he said: 'That won't do. I want to see him in one minute, I'm dying fast.' A Dr Faskally (the locum) then came and examined him; it was a desperate situation, yet for some reason the doctor had Lefley carried to his own house, where he died.

When Mary came home that evening her behaviour was confused and to some, irrational, which was to have repercussions later on. She actually stated to the doctor that she expected Lefley to claim that he had been poisoned. What was then reported about her is strange indeed. A neighbour who was trying to help made her some tea and Mary said: 'I've had nothing all day because I felt so queer.' Then she talked about making the pudding. 'He told me not to make any pudding as there was plenty cooked, but I said I always make pudding and would do so as usual.' In themselves, these two statements are quite innocuous, but in the context of the later trial they were to prove lethal to her.

At Lincoln Assizes, in May 1884, she was in the box; there was no other suspect. The police were convinced that there had been foul play and she was the only suspect. She had been charged on circumstantial evidence only and she pleaded not guilty. But then she had to listen to an astounding piece of evidence from the post-mortem. There had been a massive amount of arsenic in the rice pudding: 135 grains – a fatal dose needs only to be 2 grains. Despite the fact that some white powder found in her home was found to be harmless, witnesses were called and the trial proceeded. The strongest testimony came from William's nephew, William Lister, who recounted an argument between the couple when his uncle had taken a great quantity of ale. William came to his nephew's bed and told him that he had just attempted suicide.

Other witnesses said that they had heard Mary say that she wished her husband was 'dead and out of the way'. It was a

Lincoln Assizes. The author

tough challenge for the defence, and they failed. Mary was sentenced to death and her reply was: 'I'm not guilty and I never poisoned anyone in my life.'

There is a great deal of detail on Berry's account of the horrendous experience of carrying out her execution. Berry, new to the job and anxious to do things right, was of the opinion that he was going to hang an innocent woman. But he was a professional with a task ahead of him and he carried on. He wrote his own account of the process in his memoirs:

> To the very last she protested her innocence, though the night before she was very restless and constantly exclaimed, 'Lord, thou knowest all!' She would have no breakfast and when I approached her she was in a nervous agitated state, praying to God for salvation ... but as an innocent woman ... she had to be led to the scaffold by two female warders.

The Victorian prison, Lincoln. The author

Berry records that Mary was ill when he went to fetch her on that fateful morning. She also shouted 'Murder!' Berry wrote with feeling and some repugnance about the whole business, and at having to pinion her. Her cries were piercing as she was dragged along to the scaffold. As Berry reported: 'Our eyes were downcast, our senses numbed, and down the cheeks of some the tears were rolling.' After all, as soon as Berry had arrived at the gaol, a woman warder had said to him: 'Oh Mr Berry, I am sure as can be that she never committed the dreadful crime. You have only to talk to the woman to know that ...' Berry noted that he 'found the gaol in a state of panic' when he arrived. He recalled that the chaplain's prayers had sounded 'more like a sob' on the last morning of Mary Lefley's life.

The final irony is that, if we believe Berry, a farmer, who had been humiliated in a deal with Lefley, confessed to the poisoning on his deathbed. He said he had crept into the cottage on that day and put the poison in the pudding.

Berry had always been the kind of man who, when he eventually found his vocation, would revel in it, enjoy it to the full in terms of both inner satisfaction and in his need for acclamation and self-advertisement. Earlier in his life he had made the most of the smallest achievements, showing his ability as a 'spin-doctor' of his own status and reputation. He even had a business card produced, with delicate leaves across the card, his name beneath and his address of '1, Bilton Place, Bradford' also. The card proclaims his profession as well as his name and address: 'James Berry: Executioner' as if there were as ordinary a trade as a blacksmith or a printer at the time. But his life after his hangman years reveal a very different inner personality, more complex than one would have inferred from his public life and opinions.

Berry managed to indulge in all kinds of hobbies and part-time jobs when his career ended. He had various items as souvenirs and some of these were sold to Madame Tussaud's. He also began to take part in lecture tours, as there was always a morbid interest in the general public in the subject of execution. He moved to different addresses in the Bradford area, and he still had his wife, mother-in-law and one of his sons living with him at the time of the 1901 census. It is at this time that we begin to discern some of those deeper qualities explained at length in a vignette of him by his editor, Snowden Ward, who wrote that 'His character is a curious study – a mixture of very strong and very weak traits such as is seldom found in one person.' Ward noted something that also applied to Albert Pierrepoint later: that his wife knew little of her husband's professional activities. She said that she had lived with him for nineteen years but that she still did not really know him.

Berry had always been a man who looked to any kind of legal activity for earning a few pounds, and that habit was still with him when he was described as 'commission agent, late public executioner.' But his media career was a failure and he took to trading for small profits in retail. What began to emerge then was the drinking habit, something that became more serious as time went on. He once expressed this frankly and simply: 'I knew that it was drink that was the main support of the gallows.' What happened then is that he wrote begging letters to prison authorities and to people in high places in the prison estab-lishment, asking for his job back. But things had moved on and the general attitude was that there was no point in employing a man who had 'given them trouble.' And there were younger men coming through.

Surely one of the most dramatic and compelling stories of this complex man's life is the account of his reclamation, spiritually, after walking out of his home one day with the intention of taking his own life. He wrote in his memoirs:

> I could not have thought it possible that mortal man could become so low and depraved ... My burning conscience accused me of having wronged my family – my innocent, good and virtuous wife, and my sorely suffering children – with my carryings on in sin and wickedness. There was nothing else for it – I must put an end to my life.

What happened was that, as he sat on a railway platform, intending to throw himself from the window of a train in a tunnel between Leeds and Bradford, he began to pray for help and guidance, and a man came onto the platform who was in fact an evangelist. He sat with Berry and somehow a shared and very public prayer, with a gathering crowd, led to his being taken in for help by a man who ran a mission hall. In short, Berry found his spiritual redemption on that railway platform; his life was saved and he became a changed man.

He published one more book: a short one called Mr J Berry's *Thoughts Above the Gallows,* published in 1905. It was a tract against hanging and a clear assertion of a path to salvation, willed out of his past life, both public and private. There is a quiet desperation running through everything he wrote, but this final work maintains that thread of eccentricity that was always in him, with a discussion of one of his latest fads, phrenology.

He was then an evangelist, but the paraphernalia of his main occupation lingered on through time, a batch of his possessions being exhibited in a Nottingham junk shop in 1948, and in the 1950s, Berry's granddaughter still had some relics of Berry's to pass on.

James Berry died at Walnut Tree Farm, Bolton, Bradford, on 21 October 1913. It is entirely in keeping with the man and his character that the local obituary should contain an anecdote about Berry trying to sell the cigar case of a man he had

Charles Peace depicted in an old pamphlet. Author's collection

executed. That note of desperation and the need for small profits, while at the same time feeling a sense of the grandeur of his past, sums up one of the puzzles of Berry the hangman – a rare mix of dignity and low-life street hawking. He always looked to a quick profit and somehow, as with almost all hangmen in the records, never fully accommodated his professional self with his self-esteem.

He was a man of profound contradictions, with a reputation which attracted the media. As one journalist wrote after hearing Berry talk: 'He subsequently went a-lecturing and in that capacity introduced us to quite a modern pronunciation of the word guillotine. He called it *gelatine* . . .' They liked to laugh at him, though always with a shiver of revulsion.

CHAPTER 6

James Billington and Some Curiosities
(in office 1884–1901)

I do not declare to occupy the reader's attention with a description of Mr Billington, who is an excellent workman and has given the most perfect satisfaction to his clients. (R P Watson)

A social documentarist venturing into Newgate for some interesting 'copy' met James Billington and gave a picture of the execution shed. He noted that 'from the condemned cell to the place of execution is not more than 40 feet' and that Billington was the man impressively in control: 'I never hope to experience this awful, ignominious and brutal death ... Who knows, the writer may be a great man some day if he escapes Mr Billington ... The hanging performed by Mr Billington leaves nothing to be desired.' He sarcastically goes on to say that the dead felons, could they do so, would provide a 'certificate of merit' to the hangman. It would seem, then, that in James Billington, the first of a long dynasty of hangmen from that family in Lancashire, was most successful and that his name is not attached to any farces or bunglings.

Though a Bolton man, as Steve Fielding has written, he replaced Berry and that 'it was unusual for the normally thrifty Yorkshiremen to employ a Lancashire man, who would have to travel and therefore run up an expenses account ...' But it did happen, and for eight years he was the man who became quite a familiar sight at Armley Gaol, busy in the execution shed there.

He had been married twice, having been born in Bolton in 1847. His first wife, Alice Pennington, died in 1890, aged only forty; they had lost three children, including a little girl called Polly. One of the few anecdotes we have of him that show us the ordinary, human side of the man is the tale that, after his daughter's death, her school-friends brought a wreath for her and the future hangman was over-come with grief, saying: 'See, I'd sooner have lost £5 than ha' lost her!'

James Billington, hangman. Laura Carter

He first worked in the mills as a piecer and then he sang in clubs and pubs before entering retail trade (as many hangmen did) as a barber at Farnworth. James was, even when very young, interested in the macabre subject of execution, and he used to experiment with a dummy, done to death from a home-made scaffold constructed in the backyard where they lived at Higher Market Street in Farnworth.

As he was rooted in that community, cutting hair and no doubt chatting about holidays and work as barbers tend to do, he had to try to avoid the morbid curiosity aroused by his other job. His shop obviously attracted journalists and he tried to travel under a guise of anonymity too. He was known as Higgins when out on execution business, very smart and presentable. This would be the man met and respected by the reporter in Newgate, who had no doubt gone there partly in search of this quiet professional 'in his lair'.

He had long wanted to be a hangman, and had applied at the same time as Berry, wanting Marwood's position. He was to be in office for seventeen years from 1884 to 1901. After the application, Billington was called to York where he was inter-viewed and asked to describe what method he would use to hang people. When he first began he worked near London, employed to work in the London and Home Counties. But he started work at Armley in 1884, hanging Joseph Laycock.

Laycock was a worker at Kelham Island in Sheffield and was always a problem to someone. From being very young he lived by his fists and by indulging in petty crime. When he married Maria Green she probably had no idea what a problem she had saddled herself with, and they soon had a large family, four children born by 1884. Maria's life was desperately deprived and tough. Laycock was often away as he was a militiaman (and also sometimes behind bars) and the young wife even had to resort to collecting bottles to make ends meet.

The couple were settled in White Croft and their relationship was more than stormy – it was deathly perilous. Laycock had a homicidal streak and the local community knew that. Maria's way of coping was to drink heavily, so matters degenerated rapidly. He assaulted her and did a spell in gaol for it. But not long afterwards, two men saw Laycock early in the morning, looking agitated. Mysteriously, there was no sound from the Laycock home for some time. Neighbours and Maria's mother eventually realised that something dreadful had happened, and they saw Maria lying dead, her head almost off her shoulders. The police were called.

In the Laycock house the officers found the man with his throat cut, not dead, but wanting to expire. He had cut the throats of all four of his children. When he was well enough to stand trial, the common problem in these cases was to emerge: was he insane? Lawyers throughout the nineteenth century increasingly found themselves having to try to construct a defence of insanity in these instances, and it was always difficult to do so. In the case of Laycock, it was known that his father and his uncle had both taken their own lives. The judge was of the opinion that this was not the act of a sane man, but the jury disagreed.

Laycock's response to the death sentence was: 'Thank you, your worship, thank you.' After inspection by medical men, out to verify the point about genetic insanity, resulted in their insisting that there was no such influence in this case. He was to be a victim of Billington. It was a blessed release, one might argue. When it came near to the time he was to be taken to be hanged, his resolve weakened and he was weeping, overcome by the desperate situation, when Billington came to the cell.

Laycock asked, pleadingly, 'Thou'lt not hurt me?' The report of
the conversation was written in such a way that Billington's
Bolton accent was attempted: 'Theaull be eawt of existence in
two minutes.' But Laycock collapsed and had to be helped to
the noose. As Billington fixed the rope where he wanted it, the
condemned man spoke his last words: 'Oh my children, my
children. Lord have mercy on my children.'

Billington's record of executions went far beyond Yorkshire,
though. He was the man who hanged Amelia Dyer at Newgate,
who had murdered a four-month-old child. She had been one
of the people involved in the so-called 'baby farming' scandal
at the time, probably killing at least six babies, purely for the
money. But his most famous (or infamous) client was arguably
the poisoner, Dr Neil Cream, at Newgate, in 1892.

Mrs Dyer, the baby-farmer, being tried. From Famous Crimes *(1910).* Author's
collection

Cream was born in Scotland but he emigrated to Canada in the 1950s. After graduating in medicine he started practice in Chicago, but he was fond of using poison and had a streak of homicidal tendency in him, poisoning his mistress's husband in 1881 and when released ten years later from Joliet Prison he went to London and indulged his psychopathic desires by attracting prostitutes whom he could use for experiments with strychnine.

But the bad doctor liked notoriety and enjoyed the risk of being found – a common trait in serial killers. He even went to the police to tell them that not only was he in danger of attack but that he knew the identity of the killer who had been dubbed 'The Lambeth Poisoner' (himself of course). Not long after, following a spell back in America, he returned to London and while doing his nefarious experiments, he was described by a survivor and of course, arrested. A woman pretended to have taken pills, knowing the danger she was in, and went to fetch the law. The officers found seven bottles of strychnine at his home. The next step was to court, and after that, Newgate, to await execution.

James Billington, along with others present at the scaffold, heard the doctor say: 'I am Jack the ...' just as he was 'dropped'. But of course, he was in gaol at the time of the Whitechapel murders.

Most of Billington's hangings were full of incident, but few so chaotic as the triple hangings at Newgate in 1899 when an assistant called Warbrick and a whole crowd of warders were present at the scaffold following a brawl in the courtroom at their trial. Billington did not have a proper view of everyone involved and he pulled the lever while Warbrick was still pinioning one of the felons. The assistant fell down the trap with the three killers, and he had the wit to grab one of the pairs of legs to break his fall.

As with all the hangmen, James had to keep plying another trade, so he took a public house called the *Derby Arms* in Bolton. He married again in 1891, to a woman called Alice Fletcher, the daughter of a local greengrocer. But before we leave the account of the first Billington, there is one more job he did that has to be told. This relates to the man in Oscar Wilde's

great poem, *The Ballad of Reading Gaol*, who killed the one he
loved:

> He did not pass in purple pomp
> Nor ride a moon-white steed,
> Three yards of cord and a sliding board
> Are all the gallows need.
> So with rope of shame the herald came
> To do the secret deed.

The murderer in question whom Wilde saw and knew was
trooper Thomas Wooldridge, who had killed his wife, Laura
Ellen, by cutting her throat, at Clewer, near Windsor. James
Billington hanged Wooldridge on 7 July 1896. The soldier was
in the Royal Horse Guards, and Wilde dedicated his poem to
him:

> In Memoriam C.T.W.
> Sometime trooper of the Royal Horse Guards
> Obiit H.M. Prison,
> Reading, Berkshire
> 7th July, 1896

James' period on the Home Office list ended in 1901. There
were several other Billingtons who were hangmen in a long
dynasty, but none of them were specifically hangmen appointed
for Yorkshire as James was. But what happened was that the
family – Thomas, who died young but was assistant, John
and William – did some executions in Yorkshire. Most notable
was William, the second of James' three sons. He performed a
number of executions in his short period in office (1902–5) and
in the records of these, one in particular gives us a vivid picture
of the Billingtons at work: this was a hanging in Ruthin in
February 1903.

William Hughes had been in the Cheshire Regiment and had
served in the Empire; he returned in 1890 and worked as a
collier near Wrexham. He married Jane Williams in 1892, but
after a few years (and the death of one of his sons) matters
between them degenerated and he left her. Jane had to work as a
housekeeper and William was convicted for desertion of his
family. There was a burning jealousy in William as he knew that

his wife was now with a man called Maddocks. Intending to kill both his wife and her lover, he arrived at the Maddocks' house with a shotgun. When he learned that Maddocks was not there, he shot both barrels into his wife and then shortly after gave himself up to the police.

Ruthin Gaol is a small, oppressive place (now a crime museum) and it had a small execution shed behind. The authorities had worked out the logistics of hanging, as a contemporary account explains: 'The prisoner occupies as his death cell, two cells which had been knocked into one . . . The cell was about fifteen yards or so from the scaffold so that he had only a short distance to walk. In the wall of the prison a hole had been knocked through, which led onto the second storey of the gallows . . .'

Into this small, quiet market town came the Billington brothers, William and John. The *Denbighshire Free Press* had this account of them:

> Great curiosity was evinced both in Denbigh and in Ruthin to see the hangman Billington . . . From appearances no one would think for a moment the two quiet- looking pale-faced persons attired in dark suits, with bowler hats, were the men who would be chief actors in the launching of a human being into eternity . . . They bore absolutely no luggage . . . that had been forwarded to the prison to await them . . . upon arrival at the jail Billington had hardly put his hand upon the bell when the ever attentive warder opened the door and admitted them . . .

It must have been a difficult night, even for the two professionals, as they slept 'very close to the condemned cell where their prisoner was sleeping his last earthly sleep.' It is a small local gaol, with narrow corridors and low roofed cells and offices. It would not be going too far to imagine that they heard Hughes snore – if he slept at all that night.

But the main point here is the bland, restrained efficiency and bearing the hangmen had. The Billingtons took their trade seriously and planned everything well. The local reporter appears to have known everything they did, pointing out that Billington 'announced everything to be in perfect order before he retired early'. As for the prisoner, he simply asked for one last thing – to see a photograph of his family looking happy, and that was granted.

William's most celebrated victim was Samuel Dougal, of the Moat House Farm case in Chelmsford. Dougal had killed and buried Camille Holland at the farm and it had taken detectives a long time to find her body in a trench. The importance of that case with regard to hanging was that there was an incident on the scaffold involving the chaplain. The Rev Blakemore had a strong desire to ascertain the truth for moral and religious reasons, in his capacity of attendant chaplain. But he stepped over the line of protocol and good sense when he delayed the whole proceedings for some time, asking Dougal, who was standing on the trapdoor with the hood over his head, if he was guilty or not guilty. There was a delay, but the man was heard to say the word 'guilty' a split-second before the lever was pulled. This led to a scandal, and finally to a reform in legally-sanctioned procedure, barring chaplains from interfering with the work of professionals in the penal service. Billington must have been patient that day.

There is considerable confusion in the sources of information about William Billington, principally about his career and the main events of his life. A book printed in the 1940s has this in a chapter on executioners:

THE MADNESS OF BILLINGTON
William Billington was public executioner. In 1925 he went mad and murdered his wife and two of their children, then killing himself.

This was written by Violet Van Der Elst, a militant campaigner for the abolition of hanging. It seems that someone was in a muddle here, as that fact seems to apply to the Rochdale hang-man, John Ellis.

The main chroniclers of hangmen in Britain agree that William lived from 1873 to 1934. Yet the Billington family historian has him born in 1875, in Standish. What that historian does explain is that there were indeed family problems around William and his wife but not murder or suicide. In July 1905 he was charged with failing to maintain his wife and two children; they were taken into the Bolton workhouse as a result. He was given a month's hard labour in gaol. There was further trouble and he had a second sentence later. The real muddle comes with the note in the family history on the website that 'William died on 2 March, 1952 in his early 60s'. If he was born in 1875, that is clearly wrong.

William's life is a mystery in some ways, but what is clear in terms of the work of the Billingtons is that execution was often difficult and sometimes sensational. The most important factor is the event of 1899 in Lincoln. There, when James was booked to do a job, he was too ill and William went in his place. Amazingly, the astonished governor allowed matters to proceed. William told the governor that he had experience when in fact he had not, and was not on the official list until three years later. He had to tell the Prison Commission that he had performed an execution while not sanctioned by the Home Office.

Another Billington scandal was one involving a mysterious character called 'Warbrick' who ran a campaign of hatred against William, at one point writing to the Home Secretary, sending a newspaper cutting with an account of William being convicted for assault.

After the long career of James, the other Billingtons were involved in hangings but often as assistants. John Ellis, the Rochdale barber, came on the scene, and then the first of the Pierrepoints. But one interesting footnote is that several men applied for the post of hangman after James's retirement, including a certain Alfred Holdaway, a man who missed his place in the history of execution because his wife told him not to do it. Mrs Holdaway thought the occupation very wrong and in fact disgusting, so Holdaway went into prison service instead, working at Rampton and Broadmoor.

Alfred was a firm, upright man. His portrait shows a man of military bearing, wearing dress uniform very like worn in an officers' mess. This was his Broadmoor uniform. He had started in domestic service, and then applied for the hangman vacancy on Billington's retirement. He was actually offered the post, so

Alfred Holdaway, with his family. Author's collection

indeed would have followed the same career trajectory as Ellis, as far as we know. Success in such an application was down to character, suitable background and the right references.

Since the Aberdare Committee of the 1880s, short periods of training were brought in for aspiring hangmen. Holdaway must have had an interview but I have not been able to discover evidence of this. He was born around 1875, married twice and became a much respected officer in the particularly dangerous setting of institutions for the criminally insane. He became head warder at Broadmoor and was later sent to Rampton after a riot, to help restore order and discipline. Alfred retired from the prison service in 1932 and then from all work in 1943. In his later years he moved to Scunthorpe, where he became verger of St John's church. One piece of family oral history concerns Alfred's memories of work at Broadmoor, where he recalled that inmates doing the gardens were often well-to-do people who could very easily have been hanged: talented barristers, he claimed, had saved their lives in court, but of course the alternative was a life sentence amongst the criminally insane.

CHAPTER 7

Henry Pierrepoint

Henry worked in the gasworks and the ironworks but there were periods ... when the children had to rely on the local mission for free clogs. (Leonora Klein)

As the last century progressed, in popular culture the name Pierrepoint became synonymous with the career of public hangman. At the beginning of that dynasty, there was Henry, known to most as Harry, and he learned the trade with the Billingtons, after a proper official training for the work. But when the man from Clayton first travelled down to London to receive the full induction process at Holloway prison in 1901, he may not have realised just how much his family name was destined to be rooted in the popular imagination, and that his son would be the subject of a major film, with Timothy Spall playing the part of Albert.

The Pierrepoints began in Nottinghamshire, but they moved to Bradford and Manchester at various times. Harry's first letter of enquiry about the post of hangman was sent from Manchester: it was a simple note describing himself and saying that with regard to executioner, he had 'always had a desire for that appointment'. This is an important point, because of course the profession of hangman is one which, since its more refined and self-regarding phase after 'Long Drop' Marwood, was a pursuit offering a very welcome addition to a working man's income. Moreover, the work involved travel and of course it entailed the face-to-face meetings with national celebrities – the figures who had dominated the murder pages of the newspapers for a time and whose faces often were drawn prominently in true crime magazines. Harry certainly felt those kinds of attractions to the work.

Harry was born in 1878, and was in Manchester working with a firm of cabinetmakers on Oldham Road when he first wrote to the Home Office. Detectives soon checked him out, calling at significant addresses and asking about him. After all, there were certain undesirable types who were attracted to the work, and they had to be found out. But reports of the first Pierrepoint were favourable and he impressed Governor Cruickshank at Strangeways prison where he had first been interviewed. Cruickshank simply said: 'I have seen this man and I am of the opinion that he will make a satisfactory assistant executioner.'

Harry had not been married long, and his wife would have to know what he was planning as a parallel career to his regular work. Unlike the wife of Mr Holdaway, Mary Pierrepoint accepted the fact; she did try to dissuade him, but he went ahead. He went to London for his training and experienced a sobering taste of what the Victorian London prisons were like: he saw Newgate and Holloway, and most powerfully, he stayed in the hangman's cell at Newgate (the prison was being dismantled at the time). As Steve Fielding, the biographer of the Pierrepoints, pointed out, that room overlooked the condemned cell. That raises the important subject of the hangman's crucially important observation of his client.

The condemned had to be studied in order to ascertain size, weight, demeanour, general spirits and character. The hangman's experienced eyes would assess his victim's body weight and then know what weight to have in his sack when the drop was rehearsed. The normal procedure was for the sack to be tested at the right weight and then for the rope to be left overnight to stretch. In Harry's case, as a trainee, he also worked with a dummy in his training schedule. He had to pinion the dummy's arms and then put on the noose – all in very quick time of course. In many ways, Harry was the first hangman to undergo the new regime of methodical training, following the Aberdare reports. He was watched closely in all his training tasks, and then a brief report was written on his performance and sent to the commissioner of prisons. This noted that Harry performed all the duties and that he appeared 'an apt and promising pupil, handy and active, and taking great excitement in his early lessons at Newgate'.

There is a strong irony in that training: here was a man who was to be a professional executioner, learning the trade in the very place which had been the very heart of the nation's extremely harsh punitive regime in the days early in the previous century, when so many criminals were brutally strung up, often by bunglers. The statistics for capital punishment in the years in which Harry and his brother Tom were most active – up to c.1950 – provide an interesting contrast to those of the century before, in the 1820s. Between 1920 and 1946, 485 persons arraigned for murder were found guilty but insane. There were, of course, many reprieves. That might do something to counteract the impression that the Pierrepoints and John Ellis were hanging someone on an almost weekly basis in those years.

Nevertheless, Harry Pierrepoint was busy in that career. The start was slow and hesitant; his first contract was abortive, as the wife-killer Bill Goacher was reprieved in 1901, after being sentenced to death in Manchester. But his first actual hanging assignment came soon enough: he was engaged as assistant to James Billington to hang a Frenchman, Marcel Faugeron. Young Harry could not have asked for a more smooth and professional despatch of the man: as assistant, he had to help pinion the man's arms behind his back, then tie the straps on the man's legs at the scaffold trap, before moving gingerly back off the trapdoor. The most telling detail we have about this first job is told simply but resonantly by Steve Fieding, who notes that Dr Scott, present at this execution, approached Harry after the job, felt his pulse and said, with a smile: 'You will do.'

Harry worked with Billington again, near to his own area, in Manchester; there, they had to execute one Patrick McKenna, and that experience was very different from the hanging of the calm and collected Frenchman. McKenna was an emotional wreck; add to this the fact that Billington was clearly a very sick man when he arrived to do the work, and we can understand how tough this was for Harry Pierrepoint. McKenna wept and sobbed and called out to God. Harry learned something that day which had not been on the curriculum at the training session: this was a man, not a dummy, and he had in his own way appealed for the most humane end to his life that the professionals in judicial killing could give him. Harry understood this, and perhaps that day he learned just how quickly the strapping and the pulling of the lever had to be done: in seconds.

The other hard lesson learned that day was in the necessity of avoiding the crowds and the media; the two hangmen exited the gaol by a rear thoroughfare, and went out into the streets by way of an underground passage.

Only a few weeks after the McKenna hanging, Billington was dead, and by March 1902, Harry was asked to take up the responsibility of being chief executioner.

There are detailed lists and summaries of Harry Pierrepoint's hanging assignments, in books by Steve Fielding and by John Eddleston (see bibliography) so it is intended here to retell only the cases relating to Yorkshire or to events which highlight significant aspects of Harry's personality and professional life.

As Harry stepped into the role of chief executioner, John Ellis became one of the men who acted as his assistant; it was destined to be a relationship often under strain, but on the whole they worked well together, and teamwork was the first priority of the hangman's art in the twentieth century. Ellis was very impressed with Harry in their work together, and certainly they were busy, with twenty-five hangings taking place in the year 1902. In the next year Harry had

A suggested alternative to hanging, 1915. Daily Sketch

his first client who turned out to be a major figure in the records of infamy and homicide: Amelia Sach, a woman who ran a nursing home and who had become an operator in the nefarious trade of baby farming. Her co-offender, Annie Walters, was also heavily involved in this terrible business of killing babies who could not be found a home.

But this meant that, for the first time, Harry and William Billington would be hanging two women. Both men took time to observe the women in their separate cells, assessing weight and so on. It was to highlight a feature of the criminal justice system at the time which disturbed everyone concerned; in this case, male warders were standing by because of the fear instilled across Holloway gaol by the gallows preparations and the presence of women victims.

Baby farming had a long history; there had always been a very high death rate of children in the workhouses of the eighteenth century and there have never been statistics to state how many of these deaths may have been homicide. In the nineteenth century it became common for middle class parents to hand over children to child-minders. In 1870 there had been a major scandal when babies' bodies had been found in Lambeth and these were linked to two women, Sarah Ellis and Margaret Waters, the so-called 'Brixton Baby Farmers'. Walters and Sach were such criminal types, and there was no doubt at the trial that they were guilty. They had appeared before the famous Mr Justice Darling, described by his biographer, Dudley Barker, as 'One of the most human judges of our time, and some of his critics have said he was too human.'

The most emotionally powerful moment of the hanging ritual was when after the two women had met face to face for the first time since their trial, they were placed on the trapdoor and, as the noose and caps were put in place by Billington, Walters cried out: 'Goodbye Sach' and Sach began to collapse, losing consciousness. Harry was quick-thinking enough to move fast and grab her to support her just before she fell to her death.

Harry's Yorkshire victims were many and varied, but one of the saddest and most despicable was arguably the killer of a little girl, Mary Lynas, James Clarkson. It was a very moving case, and is more so through modern eyes, as the killer was only nineteen and the victim twelve. Clarkson had cut Mary's throat in the yard at Bennison Street, Guisborough, just after Christmas in 1903. The killer had tied her hands after death and carried the body to some fields nearby. There was so much evidence of blood on the ground and on a number of items at Clarkson's house that he was soon traced and charged. The only odd point in the trial was when Clarkson's father made the statement that his son had always been squeamish at the sight of blood. As John Eddleston has written: 'Could such an apparently delicate person have cold-bloodedly slashed a child's throat?' The jury at York thought so, and he was condemned. Certainly that was confirmed in the death cell because he constantly cried out: 'What made me do it?'

When Harry moved back to live in Yorkshire, at Clayton, he worked as a carrier. It was the right kind of move because as he has his own small firm, he could easily mix that trade with his second job and adapt to different demands when the time for hanging work came along.

His hangings in Yorkshire during his career covered almost every imaginable variety of murder. The commonest, the murder of a wife or girlfriend by the man involved, is represented by the sheer blunt murder done by Rotherham labourer, John Kay, who had simply killed his woman with a hatchet and then stopped a police officer in the street to confess. Similarly ordinary in the annals of murder was the crime committed by Edmund Hall, who had killed his father-in-law at York. For that execution, Harry had acted as assistant to John Billington; the full story of that killing entailed the melancholy account of Hall's depression, an illness intensifying since being discharged from the army; he had also suffered in an industrial accident. It became one of those difficult cases in which the killer may or may not have been of sound mind. But medical evidence suggested that Hall was on a very short fuse and was a danger to the public. However, the case seemed to be clearly one with premeditation.

The year 1904 has perhaps the most bizarre case in Harry's career as hangman. This involved Joseph Fee, a butcher from Clones in County Monaghan. His victim, John Flanagan, was found in a pile of manure near to Fee's abattoir and Fee was arrested. But Fee was tried twice before finally appearing in Belfast assizes where it emerged that there had been a motive (money). The strange events following were nothing to do with Fee. A telegram was sent to Harry at Clayton asking him to cross the Irish Sea and report to the governor of Armagh prison to do the job. But as Harry and William Billington were en route for Ireland, a man appeared at the prison and said that he was there to hang Fee. But the man knew none of the details of Pierrepoint nor anything else that might have made his ruse work. He was taken to a cell.

Fee had said repeatedly that he was innocent and that was something that naturally troubled Harry all through the preparation and observation; but at the last moment, when pinioned, the man called out: 'Executioner! Guilty!'

Harry's son, Albert, was born in February 1905 and Harry had had to travel down to London to do an execution just a week before his son's arrival. Just a short time after that, he was in London again, and his victims that time were the first convicts to be hanged on fingerprint evidence. The name of Stratton will always be linked to that massive step forward in forensic science. The Stratton brothers had killed shopkeeper Thomas Farrow and his wife in Deptford and the new fingerprint men at Scotland Yard got to work. The evidence was accepted in court; for the hangmen, it presented the essential task of making sure that the right man went onto the right rope. Albert was heavy and Alfred much lighter, so Harry had to chalk the names 'Albert' and 'Alfred' under the right nooses.

The one Leeds appointment Harry had to miss was the execution of Thomas Tattersall, who had cut the throat of his wife, Rebecca, in Wakefield. At that moment, a problem was caused by the fact that William Billington was in prison. He was separated from his wife and had not kept up his maintenance payments. That was embarrassment enough for the authorities, but then, in August 1905, they were short of assistant hangmen. The difficulty was only sorted out when a certain William Warbrick was brought out of retirement to assist John Billington. Harry and Ellis were required to attend for business at Pentonville to send Arthur Devereux to his maker for slaughtering his own family.

One of Harry's most bizarre jobs at Wakefield was the case of Thomas Mouncer. He had been sentenced to die for the killing of Elizabeth Baldwin, whom he had been living with in Middlesbrough. Mouncer had become jealous of a man she was spending time with and delivered some very direct threats. While out drinking the *ménage a trios* was stirred into dissension by the boyfriend's over zealous praise of Elizabeth.

Lord Hewart, who was involved in many high profile murder cases. Author's collection

Back home later on, Mouncer took out his rage on poor Elizabeth and next day Mouncer confessed to a murder, approaching a constable in the street. But in court, the killer made a huge attempt to argue that it had been an accidental death. His tale was that the woman had taken a knife to him; he claimed that he had taken the knife from her and then merely thrown her onto the bed. Mouncer argued that his throwing of her had killed her somehow, and so there was no premeditation. That slender and tall tale did not fool the jury. Mouncer was hanged and the men to do the job were the two Pierrepoints – two because Thomas Pierrepoint had now joined the ranks of the executioners.

CHAPTER 8

Thomas Pierrepoint

The job was not as simple as having a strong stomach – and the strength to pull a lever when it mattered. (National Archives note)

arry's brother, Thomas, joined forces to execute Harry Walters on 9 April 1906 at the point when Wakefield's facilities had been refurbished; the death cell and suite (as these areas of prisons were euphemistically termed) were on C Wing. The physical dimensions and technical areas of the scaffold were to receive much attention at various points in the history of hanging. In this instance, the suite consisted of two cells, one having been knocked through so that the condemned man could have some exercise without going out into the general yard.

These death cells were on a second floor landing. At Wakefield the whole place had been purpose built, with the section having a glass top and a beam and chain in a commodious area. A little later, there was to be a controversy about the dimensions of the trapdoor scaffold area, as we now know after the Home Office review in 1920, looking at the tendency of condemned persons hitting their heads as they were hanged (in some prisons). John Ellis was consulted, as we know from papers opened in 2005 in The National Archives, and he said that at Winchester prison in particular, the gallows trapdoors were too narrow. Ellis had recommended that these doors were too narrow and that the walk to the gallows was too long. The Winchester pit was much narrower than the one at Pentonville, for instance. This information, surfacing many years after the execution period, highlights the conditions under which the hangmen worked. Wakefield was clearly aware of the need to address the actual physical space of the scaffold.

In this new workplace the brother got to work, leaving the rope to hang and stretch overnight, after the weights and rope being ascertained. It was an auspicious start to their partnership and all went very well. Tom was adept at marking the place where the man would stand, and at coiling the noose ready for use at the required height; then both men stood by the cell ready to move their man swiftly to the platform. Walters was pinioned and dropped in seconds.

In an account of Yorkshire hangmen, the question has to arise at some point: what would happen when a man from the hangman's own town was to be executed? The answer to that is illustrated in the case of Bradford killer John Ellwood. He claimed that he knew Harry well and that when the time came, he would create major problems for the hangman. Ellwood had committed a cool and very public murder. He had returned to the office where he had formerly worked, in Bradford, and timed his arrival when there would be cash on the premises.

Ellwood had left the firm, Fieldhouse and Jowett, six months previously. He had had a heated row with his employers and had left under a cloud; it was therefore not hard for the police to show that, as an employee, he would know the routine of the place in a typical week, and would therefore be aware that large amounts of money were brought to the building by the company every Friday. It was hardly going to be a problem for the investigating officers, to find the man who had beaten Tom Wilkinson to death with a poker in that office. There was plenty of blood on Ellwood's clothes when he was arrested, and his pathetic excuse that this was caused by a bleeding nose was not going to fool anyone. The murder scene that day had been observed by a passer-by, to whom Ellwood had vainly tried to lie that he (Ellwood) had only called there to try to obtain his job back and that someone else must have been there in a murderous frame of mind. In court, there was evidence of a letter written by Ellwood saying that he would call that day.

The trial at Leeds was spoiled by a technicality, but he was convicted of murder, and then went to appeal. The last-ditch attempt to save his neck was dramatic in the extreme; on 20 November, 1908, the applicant for Ellwood, Gregory Ellis, argued that at the trial there had been no motive for the murder satisfactorily stated or explained. A supposed letter from Wilkinson, asking Ellwood to come and discuss the reinstatement, had been dismissed and the defence team at the appeal brought this up again. It all came to nothing. The judges were convinced that Ellwood had gone to the office that day with the attention to rob and to kill, if necessary.

On 3 December 1908, Ellwood had an appointment with the Pierrepoints. The killer had openly bragged that he would create a stir on the fateful day. They had to come up with a contingency plan, and it was decided that two guards walking with the group to the scaffold would stand on planks at either side of Ellwood to restrain him when trouble started. That would mean using the hood and pinions as he struggled or kicked. But the most successful move was that the brothers had the man pinioned in the cell, taking him by surprise. There was no trouble after that, apart from the man's shouts that he was innocent, even directing one call to his hangman: 'Harry, you're hanging an innocent man!' After that, both brothers being convinced that he was not telling the truth, the only other words spoken by Ellwood, seconds before he dropped, were: 'It's too tight.'

Tom, like his brother, had written the usual application, made after John Billington's death at Harry's urging. Tom was interviewed and then went for the training at Pentonville. Of course, he had had some extra tuition from Harry and was well prepared. It seems that Tom was a 'natural' at the work, and he very smoothly adapted to work well with his brother. They were to be severely tested by one of the most bizarre executions ever done, and that was the hanging of Richard Heffernan, in Dublin, in 1910. The scene that was to emerge was one of tragic-comedy, but very dark comedy nevertheless.

Heffernan had killed a girl named Mary Walker, stabbing her and then telling people that he had seen the murder. But fate had a string of stressful incidents lined up for the Pierrepoints. First, something happened that illustrates the essential need for the hangman to protect the privacy of his identity. For some reason unknown at the time, Harry's name was on the passenger list of the ferry they were taking from Holyhead. People obviously began to take a vicarious and morbid pleasure in knowing who he was; the public hangman was always a figure of intense media interest. Wisely, he was given a private place to hide in for the journey.

The next incident in the Heffernan fiasco was that the condemned had been so unbalanced and determined to flout the hangman that he had set about clawing at his own throat to take his own life. In normal practice, suicide was high on the agenda of a hanging in the planning of the official personnel involved. The man was sedated and put on close guard. The brothers were aware that this was a highly unusual and challenging case. They knew that they would not only have to be acutely aware of the need for precise attention to all safety procedure, but that the victim was likely to do the most unexpected things at any time.

There were priests in attendance and they came to speak with the brothers on the night before the hanging; no doubt there was extended discussion of Heffernan's condition. What Harry must have noticed – and it became important the next day – was that there was a very small space on the trapdoor area by the

Plan of Kilmainham. Author's collection

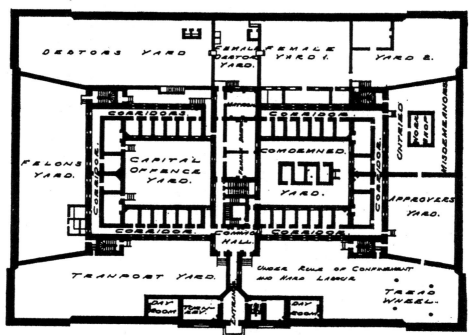

drop. What happened there the next day was that the con-demned man strode into the trapdoor area with a gaggle of priests; he was weeping and praying and kissing the cross. But speed was the first consideration here, and even when Tom did his pinioning well and stood back, there were the priests, still on the trapdoor. There was no alternative: decorum must be broken, and the priests pushed hard out of the way. That's what Harry did, and then down went the lever.

There was controversy in Harry's life not long after this, and it led to his dismissal. The fuss began at an execution in Chelmsford at which the sensitive subject of the hangman's need for drink arises. The fact is that Harry arrived to do the work, with Ellis as assistant, and he had taken a drink or two. It seems that, according to Ellis in a letter to the Prison Com-missioners, that Harry had threatened violence to him: ' . . . he threatened what he would do for me, made a rush at me, but the chief warder and gatekeeper intervened and talked to him . . .' Ellis added: 'He is the first person that has ever assaulted me in all my life.' He said that he and the prison officials felt that Harry had needed drink in order to do execution work. By July 1910, Harry's name was taken from the official list of execu-tioners.

The sign that Harry was being phased out was when Tom stepped into the chief executioner's role; this was a job at Holloway. But in 1910, Tom handled his first Yorkshire execu-tion at Armley: the hanging of John Coulson. This has to be the most clear-cut and uncomplicated murder case in Yorkshire. Coulson walked around his workplace showing off a summons he had concerning violence to his wife and written on that paper was a statement that he had killed her. Suspicions were aroused and later, a constable found Jane dead at the family house, and Coulson in a deranged state, insisting that he had tried to take his own life. This had happened in Bradford so, again, Tom was in action in his own home town, among people he knew and who knew him.

Tom carried out the execution smoothly and swiftly. The most informative detail in the Coulson case, however, was in the ruse Tom came up with to slip away from the gaol unseen. He and the assistant, William Warbrick, pretended to be journalists and walked through the crowd, notebooks held prominently.

In 1911 Harry tried to put things right with the authorities, writing a long explanatory letter to the Prison Commissioners with reference to the Chelmsford affair. Harry included an implication that Ellis was acting unfairly, to 'do Harry out of work'. He insisted that the report on Chelsmford was a lie and that Harry could have reported Ellis many times for various infringements. The letter ends with a note of special pleading:

> I have a wife and five young children to keep and I can assure you I have had a lot to bear. I should be pleased if you would communicate with the Rev Benjamin Gregory of the Huddersfield Mission and enquire about me since I came to Huddersfield this last few months.

There was no reply. Obviously, there was no going back and certainly no second chance. Tom Pierrepoint was now the 'number one' and he had plenty of work in 1913. What is noticeable in that busy year is that normally Ellis and Tom worked separately, with different assistants. On just one occasion – in Worcester in June – Ellis was chief and Tom the assistant. It seems that there was tact and diplomacy at work, and in the Yorkshire hangings in the years from 1913 onwards it was usually William Willis or Albert Lumb who worked with Tom, although Tom did act as assistant on several occasions to Ellis in other counties, notably in the hanging of the famous George Joseph Smith, at Maidstone, in 1915.

Smith was the notorious 'Brides in the Bath' murderer who had drowned three of his wives and tried to make these appear to be accidental. Even the skills of the highly talented barrister, Sir Edward Marshall Hall, could not help Smith escape the noose on the charge of the murder of Bessie Mundy. Smith had also had the great forensic scientist, Sir Bernard Spilsbury, pitted against him; he had studied the deaths and made it clear that they had been faked to appear accidental. The jury took only half an hour to find him guilty, but the real drama was to come on the day of his execution, as Tom and Ellis found out.

Sir Edward Marshall Hall. Author's collection

Smith, during his trial, said at one point: 'You may as well hang me at once, the way you are going on . . . go on, hang me at once and be done with it.' He was prescient indeed: in a state of complete collapse, he was handled delicately by Tom and Ellis.

Tom was to be hangman until 1946 and his work included several high-profile cases, but his brother Harry was increasingly desperate after his dismissal. What he did in 1922 sums up a tendency in most hangmen at some point in their careers: a need to earn some money from their notoriety. Berry and Binns had certainly done that. But now, Harry Pierrepoint wrote his memoirs for a magazine, *Reynolds News*. The articles were headed, 'Ten years as Hangman'. It was to be one of the last events in Harry's life, as he died on 14 December 1922, at forty-eight. Once a hangman 'went public' he was expected to be a public commentator on all things criminal and legal and Harry would no doubt have done such things had he lived. But we are left with only those reminiscences.

It would be too optimistic to expect executioners to theorize for long on any philosophical perspective on their trade, but at least Harry did state boldly that he 'loved' his work on the scaffold. He wrote: 'It was my whole desire to become an expert official which I did through my own energies.' Hangmen tend to either explain their lives in religious ways or simply understate matters and take the line that 'somebody has to do it'. With Harry Pierrepoint is was a case of plain speaking and not much more. That makes a sharp contrast with the later memories of John Ellis, who was more loquacious and forthcoming with a neat and effective turn of phrase.

Tom Pierrepoint was to have a long period in office, from 1906 to 1946, and his work covered some major cases and also hangings of spies. Arguably, however, his most poignant execution had a Yorkshire connection, though his victim was a Lincolnshire woman, Ethel Major. He hanged another woman, Charlotte Bryant, at Exeter; both women were sentenced to death for murder by poisoning of their husbands. Just before Christmas 1934, Tom Pierrepoint, assisted by his nephew Albert, hanged Ethel Major at Hull Gaol. It was a traumatic experience for all the professionals involved but especially so for the man who had to pull the lever on the scaffold.

Ethel Major, living in Kirkby-on-Bain, not far from Lincoln, had a husband who was having an affair; she was a complex personality, tending to express herself in unconventional ways and to some she seemed naïve. She had had a child out of marriage, during the Great War, and then Arthur Major had married her. Ethel was from a rural family; her father was a gamekeeper. In many homes at that time there was strychnine used for various things, along with other poisons (the commonest being arsenic on fly-paper) and when Arthur was taken seriously ill, plain forensic work pointed the finger at Ethel, as she had the means and the motive.

Ethel Major. Laura Carter

There had been widespread debate on the issue of capital punishment in the early 1930s; one reason for this was the reprieve of a teenager sentenced to hang after a double shooting in Waddingham in Lincolnshire. But also there was the issue of hanging women and also the difficult topic of diminished responsibility. It would be useful and interesting for the public to know how the executioner stood on the matter and, unusually, Tom gave an interview to the *Yorkshire Post* in February 1930. Typically, he was interviewed doing his 'day job' at a foundry. His views were simple and direct: 'I think it would be encouraging people to murder if the death penalty were abolished, but it would make no difference to me either way.' Steve Fielding makes it clear that Tom put financial gain before moral debate, however.

His resolve was certainly tested in the Major case. Young Albert had applied for the executioner post in 1931, stressing that his father had taught him well. He was twenty-six at the time and had been brought up largely in Huddersfield, where his father had at times worked at the gasworks. The new Pierrepoint team of Tom and Albert arrived at Hull and made ready to attend to Ethel Major. They would have known the salient points of the case – mainly that a dog had died, as well as Mr Major – but they would not have known how complex the whole affair had been and how it was to influence thought on capital punishment.

The preparation to hang Ethel major must have been highly unusual for Tom. She was a very tiny woman, only just under

five feet tall and weighing only 122 lb. Images of her available
show her wearing unflattering glasses and an apron. She had
not spoken for herself at the trial and revisions of the case show
how terrible was her ordeal, but to the last she was calm, and it
appears that she was an 'ideal client' for the Pierrepoints, going
stoically to her fate. Young Albert was naturally intrigued by the
thought of hanging a woman, as there was an emotional impact
involved that needed some reflection. John Ellis spoke at length
about his hanging of Emily Swann and Edith Thompson, and
he could not resist talking at length about the sense of moral

The graveyard for hanged convicts, Lincoln. The author

The graveyard in full view. The author

outrage involved in hanging a female. But apparently Tom Pierrepoint knew the score when it came to the gallows for a woman victim. He reassured Albert that she would be controlled and said: 'I shall be very surprised if Mrs Major isn't calmer than any man you have seen so far.'

For Tom Pierrepoint, two days in January 1919, was busy in seeing to the death of three soldiers. It had been the tail-end of the war and offences were common as men returned home to face all kinds of relationships problems; there was also a spate of crimes of violence often linked to ex-servicemen. The three hangings involved an assistant we know little about – Robert Baxter.

Mrs Van Der Elst in protest outside a prison. Author's collection

Benjamin Benson was the first to hang, on 7 January. He had been having an affair with a married woman, Annie Mayne, in Hunslet, Leeds. She was married to Charles Mayne but he had left her when her affair with Benson began and he found them together one day. Benson moved in to live with Annie, but she was a promiscuous type and had other male friends. Benson came home one day and Annie came home with a young soldier, taking him upstairs. Benson went to them and the soldier fled. But after that there was a confrontation and he hit Annie. The argument escalated into extreme violence and Benson took a razor and slashed her throat.

The following day Tom executed two young soldiers who had murdered a shopkeeper in Pontefract. These men were Percy Barrett and George Cardwell; they had murdered Rhoda Walker at Town End and then pawned some of the goods, even giving some jewellery to Cardwell's mother in Halifax. They

Mrs Van Der Elst's car being obstructive in an anti-hanging protest. Author's collection

went to London, but the pawn tickets, as in so many cases, made it easy to track them down. They said they were innocent, right to the moment they stood on the trap.

The inter-war years were a time of prolonged and heated debate on all aspects of the criminal law. There had been two significant pieces of legislation which influenced homicide decisions, one in 1908 which raised the minimum age of execution from sixteen to eighteen, and the 1922 Infanticide Act which made that offence a variety of manslaughter rather than murder. Then, just before the hanging of Ethel Major, in 1931, there was the Sentence of Death (Expectant Mothers) Act in which pregnant women after giving birth were reprieved. Previously there had been the 'pleading of the belly' which meant that it would be a stay of execution if a woman were pregnant at time of trial.

These were all humane measures, long overdue, but the persistent problems were the nature of insanity in homicide, with the idea of diminished responsibility, and the difficult nature of a whole range of illnesses which an offender might be suffering from. The Ronald True case of 1922 had an impact on the subject, largely because he had been, in the opinion of the press, 'reprieved by the doctors' and he was wealthy, having powerful friends. Harry Pierrepoint, just before his death, commented to the press that there was a gross disparity in that, as another man, with a similar 'crime of passion' was hanged, and he had been poor. The papers talked about 'trial by Harley Street' and the *Evening News* wrote:

> Mr Justice Avory's terse and mordant comment on leaving the law to Harley-Street experts shows the country where it stands under a Home Secretaryship that says, 'I am powerless when the doctors have spoken.' All you have to do after a trial, then, is to call in the pathologist, get his certificate, and leave that to confirm or reverse the verdict!

In 1923 writers to *The Times* on the debate made points which express common feelings at the time; one writer made the point: 'Now what is our machinery? The judge has no option. With due solemnity, he passes sentence of death equally upon

The reply to a Van Der Elst letter from the Bishop of Durham. Author's collection

the miserable mother and upon the callous ruffian.' Another writer noted that in his opinion, there was 'a growing feeling in the country against capital punishment ... there is an immense body of silent opinion against it ...'

The year following there was a deputation to the Home Secretary pressing for the abolition of hanging. The groups involved included the Society of Friends, the Women's Co-operative Guild and the Howard League for Penal Reform. The leading figures were George Lansbury, Major Christopher Lowther and Margery Fry. One of the most strident voices against the death penalty was the campaigner Violet Van Der Elst, a wealthy woman with land and status in rural Lincoln-shire who made a habit of driving her large and showy motor vehicle to the prisons where executions were to take place and protest in front of the growing crowds of onlookers.

The hangmen carried on in spite of all the debate and dis-agreement, but of course, their written statements were valu-able documents for both sides. Also in the picture were accounts of the alternatives to hanging, such as the campaign by Elbridge Gerry, founder of the NSPCC, to replace the noose with 'humane' electric death. He wrote many articles on cruelty and capital punishment.

In 1930 there was a Select Committee on Capital Punish-ment, led by Sir John Power. The crime of murder was the only issue, as since 1838 the only executions had been for that crime. The conclusion was that: 'The witnesses felt bound . . . to point out that in their view the risks to which the officers of the law were exposed in the discharge of their duties would be en-hanced if capital punishment were abolished' and furthermore, that: 'professional burglars and criminals of that type did not normally carry lethal weapons in this country and that was directly attributable to the gallows . . .'

One of the spin-off effects of this new caution and reflection was the nature of recruitment to the ranks of hangman. The Aberdare Report of the 1880s had involved the testimonies of medical men such as this, and it was a sobering exercise for all concerned:

I descended immediately into the pit where I found the pulse [of the hanged Man] beating at the rate of 80 to the minute, the wretched man struggling desperately to get his hands and arms free. I came to this conclusion from the intense muscular action in the arms, fore arms and hands, contractions, not continuous but spasmodic, not repeated with any regularity but renewed in different directions and with desperation. From these signs I did not anticipate a placid expression in the face and I regret to say my fears were correct. On removing the white cap about one and a half minutes after the fall I found the eyes starting from the sockets and the tongue protruded, the face exhibiting unmistakeable evidence of intense agony.

As a result of this, and of Binns's blunders, things began to change. In addition to the expertise of the hangman, after 1913, the medical men present at an execution played their part in ascertaining the length of the drop. There is a difference in the tables of drops for 1892 as compared with 1913; for instance, the average range of weight, say 135–145 lb, differs by almost a foot deeper drop in 1913. Authorities were taking no chances. There was much more consideration for ensuring a swift exit.

Albert, the last and most celebrated of the Pierrepoint hangman family, applied at a time when the results of these deliberations had an effect on recruitment.

CHAPTER 9

Albert Pierrepoint
(in office 1932–1956)

If I can give them the respect and dignity at the last moment, that's my job and I come away satisfied.

The name of Albert Pierrepoint has almost become the definitive term that follows if the topic of hangmen comes up in conversation; in recent years it has been a such a topic, largely because Timothy Spall played Albert in a major motion picture in 2006. That film, and the media interest it generated, gave massive attention to the lives and motivations of the hangmen and it gave audiences something of the Yorkshire context. After all, most of the famous hangmen have been northerners – from Lancashire or Yorkshire – and speculation on why that is the case has always been popular.

Albert's time as chief executioner includes such large slices of crime history as the hanging of Ruth Ellis, the traitor Lord Haw Haw, various German spies, the Nuremburg executions, Derek Bentley, John Christie and Timothy Evans. In all he hanged around 433 men and 17 women and served from 1932 to 1956. Pierrepoint died in Southport in 1992, aged eighty-seven. He wrote his autobiography, but we also have two recent works on his life: Steve Fielding's *Pierrepoint: A Family of Executioners* and Leonora Klein's *A Very English Hangman*.

Albert's progress towards stepping into the shoes of his father and uncle followed the usual course, writing the letter and then being called for interview at Strangeways. He had looked closely at his father's notes on the profession and was fully informed when he went to be considered. His letter of acceptance came with a list of rules, and the tone of these is very much a sign of a regime 'under new management' in the sense that there is a great deal of stipulation of conduct and procedure. Most of the rules are concerned with punctuality and discretion; one of the most telling sections reads: 'he [the hangman] should avoid attracting public attention in going to or from the prison, and he is forbidden from giving to any person particulars on the subject of his duty for publication.' The spirit of the rules is in line with the renewed demands for moral probity and sensitivity on the part of the hangmen added to the list.

One man who had recently resigned from the list, Tommy Mann, was still around to advise writers on the Pierrepoints when Klein wrote her life of Albert, and he was one of the select names on the list, only finishing that work because of the demands of his main employment.

For Albert, his first job teamed up with Tom was in Ireland. The two men crossed to Dublin where there was a victim waiting for them at Mountjoy Prison. Steve Fielding makes a point that Tom had a revolver and bullets in his belongings before that trip – hardly a feature we might have expected in that trade – but in that instance there had been trouble over in Ireland regarding the killer, Patrick MacDermott, who had been sentenced to die for the murder of his brother. It appears that his motive was to inherit the land where they had a farm, in Roscommon. The journey the hangmen took to Ireland on that occasion was as eventful and tense as anything in a crime novel; they had to make three changes of transport, then take the Holyhead ferry again. As Tom was a good singer, he joined in with a party on the ship, and later there was a gang of people waiting for their arrival in Dun Laoghaire. It was only because a man they had befriended gave them cover and a lift that they escaped trouble. The execution went smoothly, but there was another crowd waiting for them outside the gaol; it seems that Tom was an expert at melting anonymously into a group of people and he did so again, keeping his nephew under his wing. A significant footnote to the adventure (with Harry in mind) is that Tom refused the traditional whisky after the drop, when the corpse was inspected by the doctor and the good job well done celebrated with a drink.

Tom and Albert had another sixteen years in which they acted together from time to time; their joint operations are well documented, but the events which are not so well known are the reprieves. The first case Albert was supposed to watch, simply as an observer, turned out to be cancelled as a reprieve came, and a far more notorious case came along in 1936. This was the story of William Edwards of Bradford. He was sentenced to death for killing his girlfriend but he had severe epilepsy and there was ample evidence of his mental problems to make it a complex case at trial. A highly regarded doctor from Switzerland gave a statement to the effect that there was a case for diminished responsibility for Edwards. He said: 'From the facts put before me, and the examination I have made of the prisoner, I have arrived at the following conclusion, namely, that it is highly probable that Edwards suffers from occasional attacks of epilepsy.' He listed frequent headaches, moodiness and loss of temper, a history of attacks of an epileptic nature, and loss of memory.

On the fateful night, Edwards had gone out with his girlfriend and everything had been fine; they had been to the pictures in Bradford. But later, when they met again, he took out his penknife and, according to one statement, 'whirled his arm, not knowing where it fell'. But Edwards had done a similar attack previously. Eventually he was sentenced for murder and was on his way to the Pierrepoints when the reprieve came.

One hanging the two men did do together at Armley was that of David Blake, who had strangled Emily Yeomans in Middleton Woods, near Beeston. Emily was a waitress who lived near Dewsbury Road. The killer went for a heavy drinking session with Albert Schofield (his intended best man) and then went walking with Emily. Blake was hardly discreet in keeping his terrible act quiet; he gave a powder compact belonging to Emily to the wife of a man who had put him up for the night and he made a point of talking about the murder case as reported in the local paper. He was questioned by police and traces of Emily Yeoman's hair were found on him.

There was a chance that he may have been innocent, as police had arrested a man called Talbot and there was forensic evidence to link him to Emily. But it was Blake who went to the gallows.

During the Second World War there would be spies as well as murderers as clients for the Pierrepoints. At Wandsworth in 1941 they had their first such case when they hanged two Germans – Karl Drucke and Werner Walti – who had landed near Banff in Scotland. The men aroused suspicion by their general behaviour and, when accosted and searched, Drucke was found to have a pistol, a radio transmitter – and a German sausage! In July 1942, the first Englishman to be hanged for treason was a client of Tom Pierrepoint at Wandsworth: this was George Armstrong, from Newcastle.

In 1941, on 31 October, Albert Pierrepoint acted as chief executioner for the first time, and his client was an infamous London villain whose case went to the House of Lords. This was Antonio Mancini, known as 'Babe'. The killing was an ignominious one, simply a fight in relation to the club which Mancini managed, the *Palm Beach* in Soho. Mancini had been threatened after a scrap with a gang of men who he barred, one of whom was Harry Distleman. When they renewed acquaintance in a fight, Mancini had a knife ready. There would obviously be a claim for self-defence on the part of Mancini.

Even though the appeal went to the Lords, the cards were stacked against Mancini; he had a long list of previous convictions for assault and he had carried the knife ready for the encounter. It was at this job, in Pentonville, that Albert met his assistant, Steve Wade. There was no doubt that Albert had learned his trade, as he was already working out the drop when he was asked by a member of staff what might be required. New ropes from the official suppliers were ready, and the hangmen carried out the normal test-drop. This time it was Albert who was the master, with a student, Steve Wade, who was new to the game and needed guidance. They were up at 6.00 am on the morning of the hanging and Wade checked the trapdoors. Albert had given close attention to every part of the preparation, all in order to cut seconds off the execution time.

Mr Justice Hawkins wearing the black cap. From Famous Crimes *(1910).*
Author's collection

Steve Wade put the cap on Mancini and Albert turned to look at the prisoner. As the noose was put on, Mancini said: 'Cheerio.' Albert had certainly impressed the prison staff and his speed and efficiency were noted. He and Wade worked very well together, as Albert's memoirs show.

In Yorkshire, one of Albert's first tasks was to hang Sidney Delasalle, who had shot Ronald Murphy at the North Country Camp, in February 1944. This was one of those rare cases in which there was a slight possibility of the killer being in a condition of automatism, which, if proved satisfactorily by medical experts, could constitute a defence and a shift from murder to manslaughter.

Delasalle, a soldier at the North Country Camp, was in a very bad mood one day when Flight Sergeant Murphy and Corporal Taylor came to inspect the beds in Delasalle's quarters; the man was aggressive and actually challenged Murphy to go outside for a fight. That was the last straw and Murphy put the man on a charge. He did fourteen days of 'jankers'. When he came out, the revenge was vicious and swift. A line of men were queuing for tea when Delasalle appeared on the scene with a rifle. He shot Murphy several times and was then overpowered.

Clearly, there was no doubt of his guilt, but at the trial in Leeds a Dr Macadam brought up the subject of the possible automatism that may have applied to Delasalle. This is the defence made when it is demonstrated that a killer was in a trance or sleepwalking when a homicide was committed. If so, in this case Delasalle would genuinely have had no memory of what he had done. It all came to nothing; such a defence is extremely difficult to demonstrate conclusively to a jury of course.

The soldier was hanged at Durham in March, 1944.

Another wartime Yorkshire murder that led to work at the scaffold for Albert (and this time with a new assistant, Herbert Harris) was yet another killing by army men. It took place at the *Nags Head,* Clayton Heights, Bradford, in September 1944. Arthur Thompson, a soldier, and Thomas Thompson, were regulars at the pub. Arthur had made it plain to his friend that he was desperate for money, and yet one day he went to the Westwood Hospital and paid off some debts to his cronies. He was doing dangerous and risky things, including going AWOL from the army. He went on a crime spree across the Pennines, but he also did the thing that most often ends up with the police at the door: he sold some of the items stolen from Jane Coulton at the *Nag's Head.*

What Thompson had done was break into the inn and stolen money and jewellery. It seems as though Jane had been woken up and disturbed him, and she had been strangled in her bed. The forensics showed that specimens of a different blood group from Jane were present in the room at the scene where there had been a struggle in the bed. This was group A and tallied with Thompson's blood.

The killer was caught trying to sell another piece of jewellery in Overton. The police were called and the man, with false papers on him with the name of Reid, was arrested. Other items stolen from Jane Coulton were found hidden in the police car in which he was taken to be questioned.

Albert Pierrepoint was by that time an expert in his profession; he had been busy with traitors and was soon to be in demand at the trials of Nazis, for war crimes. But first we must recall his execution of one of the most notorious traitors in any nation's history, the so-called Lord Haw Haw, William Joyce. Early in the Second World War, the Nazi regime had established a widespread propaganda network, including the provision of English-speaking staff at radio Berlin. In addition to that, the Germans must have been stunned at their good fortune in having an ex-Blackshirt British fascist, William Joyce, working for them with his nickname of Lord Haw Haw. He had said that he would go to Germany (even before the war began) and 'throw in his lot' with them. Joyce was treated with a certain degree of suspicion as he may have been a double agent. But a man working for Goebbels' propaganda machine supported Joyce, against the odds, and he was accepted. Soon his broadcasts, beginning with 'This is Germany calling' and expressed in a cut-glass accent, were becoming familiar everywhere. He also began writing scripts for other radio outfits which were part of the German initiatives of psychological warfare.

Lord Haw Haw (William Joyce). Author's collection

Joyce was born in New York in 1906, the son of an Irish father and English mother. At school in Galway he had his nose broken in a fight and that affected his enunciation, giving the nasal quality to his broadcast voice later on; but he was to turn out a fit, athletic man and found an outlet for his aggression and his politic in British fascism. He even led one group of fascists into a confrontation at Lambeth Bath Hall and at that place he was cut along the face and so had a scar – something always prominent in images of him later on.

Naturally, Joyce supported the Fascists established under Oswald Mosley and lasted there until 1937, leaving them under a cloud. Under a threat of internment, he crossed to Germany in August 1939. From there his life and work led inevitably into a life as a traitor to Britain, his last broadcast being made from Hamburg in April 1945. He was arrested and charged with treason and sentenced to death, having been caught near the Danish border. He drew a swastika on the wall of the death cell and was without remorse to the end, even when he knew about the concentration camps.

Joyce's trial at the Old Bailey lasted three days. It was a hard task to demonstrate the offence of treason and, in the end, everything depended on the date his British passport expired. As it expired after his first broadcasts, he had committed treasonable offences. He even had his appeal go to the House of Lords. But on 3 January 1946, Albert, assisted by Alex Riley, hanged Lord Haw Haw.

Of course, Albert was very much in demand at the war crimes trials in Nuremberg. There had been a long period before these trials began, as the great powers and the leaders disagreed at first about the required methods of dealing with Nazis. The crimes were in a range of areas, principally in theft of works of art and, naturally, in the extermination of Jewish peoples and others in their policy of genocide. Churchill at first wanted a select (and large) number of Nazis shot without trial. The American regime considered plans such as converting the whole of Germany into a pastoral economy with no armaments at all. Largely due to the machinations of Stalin and a series of meetings to discuss trials, the long sequence of war crimes trials began and Albert Pierrepoint was to find himself at the centre of a controversy.

Much of this was related to the events developing as part of the retribution given, coming from the understandably deep hatred and vengeance in so many people. George Orwell, in his column *As I Please*, on 9 November 1945, wrote, after seeing

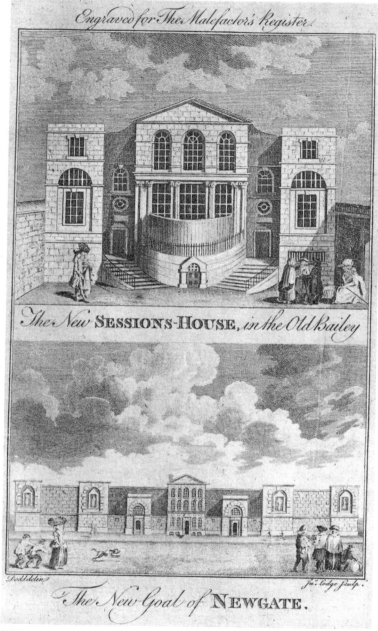

The Old Bailey Sessions House, from an old print. Author's collection

a man kicking a prostrate German prisoner: 'I wondered if the Jew was getting any real kick out of this new-found power that he was exercising. I concluded that he wasn't really enjoying it and that he was merely ... telling himself that he was enjoying it.'

In other words, when the question of a trial came up, the allied powers had to be careful that they were not as barbaric as the Nazi culprits had been in their phase of power. What happened was that a Royal Warrant allowed for the trial of some of the Belsen camp criminals under the military court system. The men on trial included such notorious Nazis as Kramer, who had been in charge at Birkenau when 200,000 Jews were gassed. This particular trial, of the Belsen Nazis, took over fifty days; at the end, the death sentences were passed, most notably including Josef Kramer, Irma Grese and Juana Bormann. Albert was the man to see these sentences carried out, being flown out there from RAF Northolt to Germany. As biographer Leonora Klein points out, there was a media frenzy at Northolt (so much for secrecy and discretion): 'For the first time in modern history, the hangman was officially embraced by the British state.'

Waiting their fate in Hameln were thirteen Nazis. Albert was to be housed away from the prison, but he obviously spent time preparing for the job. In his own autobiography he wrote about this, even to the point of the loud and constant sound of the graves being dug outside. The most challenging part of his role, however, was that he had to weigh and study each person – not his common practice in his normal work in Britain. He had a translator and spent time with each one, even with the three women who would be his victims. It was highly unusual for Albert. For one thing, he was aware that the people waiting to die would hear the traps slamming near to them as the first Nazis went to their deaths. Albert decided to hang the women first, singly, and then have double executions after that.

The bare statistics of Albert's work as executioner in the period between the end of December 1945 and October 1948 were that he hanged 226 people, and of these, 191 were Nazi war criminals or other individuals guilty of the capital crime of treason. The controversy was partly to do with something historian Sadkat Kadri notes: 'The executions themselves were reportedly even more unpleasant than such things are by their nature. Several of the men are said to have had their faces battered by the swinging trapdoor as they fell. Some thrashed around for up to fifteen minutes, suffocating at the end of nooses that had been cut too short to snap their necks.' That criticism does not apply to Albert Pierrepoint. He would not have allowed such things. In his own memoirs he writes: 'I came back to the corridor to pinion Klein, then brought him to the execution chamber . . . I adjusted the ropes and flew to the lever . . . This first double execution took just twenty-five seconds.'

It must have been a bizarre experience for Albert to return to 'normality' after that, and to turn up at various English gaols to hang common murderers rather than mass murderers of the Nazi regime. But one of his most significant jobs has a strong Yorkshire connection: the hanging of John Reginald Christie at Pentonville in July 1953. Christie, the beast of 10 Rillington Place, had strangled several women at that address (no longer in existence) and buried them on his property. Christie was born in Boothtown, Halifax, close to the Dean Clough area. When he moved to London he became a special constable and

Review of 'Yield to the Night'. Scunthorpe Telegraph

DIANA WITHOUT GLAMOUR
Outstanding in 'most gruesome' film

BRITAIN last night presented the most harrowing picture so far shown at the 1956 Cannes film festival when "Yield to the Night," in which Diana Dors plays a murderess in the condemned cell, was given its world premiere.

The blonde star was cheered by 3,000 people as she left the floodlit Festival Palace in her turquoise car matching her turquoise mink stole and sequinstudded evening gown.

She told reporters: "This is the part I have been waiting for, and it has taken me nearly 10 years to achieve it.

Film experts among the

— as she appears in the film.

— as she is usually seen.

audience of 1,800 producers and technicians from 34 countries described the slowly unwinding tale of a

woman's last days under sentence of death in a British gaol as the most gruesome shown at Cannes.

CONTROVERSY

They said Miss Dors, cast as a woman torn between desire to justify her crime and fear of the price she must pay, gave the outstanding performance of a career so far built on her success as a glamour girl.

They also praised the sensitive acting of Yvonne Mitchell as a prison guard.

Members of the British film industry said the picture, to be shown in London soon, is bound to revive public controversy over capital punishment.

used his air of authority, along with his supposed medical skills, to lure women to their doom by means of his self-made gassing equipment.

Christie, known in Halifax in his youth as 'Johnny No-Dick', clearly had profound sexual problems which had a deleterious effect on his self-esteem and played a major part in the development of his psychopathic tendencies.

A man called Beresford Brown, living near Christie's lair, found a body when he knocked through a wall. From that point, the hunt was on for the killer, and on 31 March, a police constable walking on the embankment near Putney Bridge, questioned a man hanging about, looking dishevelled. Although the man said he was one John Waddington, when he took off his hat, the officer saw that he was the wanted man, Christie. He confessed to the killings, stating that he had used a ligature to strangle his victims.

At the trial in June 1953, Christie's defence put up the argument (only to be expected) that he was guilty but insane. But that plea was dismissed and he was found guilty of murder. Naturally, with such a notorious client, there was a massive crowd gathered at Pentonville to be present at the momentous time when the 'beast of Rillington Place' would meet his doom. Harry Smith was assisting Albert that day and, as they passed a window from where they could see the crowd, Albert said: 'I suppose that's the sort of lot who watched hangings at Tyburn, with blokes selling sweets and hot rum to the crowd!'

Christie went to his death with a sneer on his face. As the hood was slipped on, Albert sensed something, and this, as he explained later, was that: 'It was more than terror ... at that moment I know that Christie would have given anything in his power to postpone his own death.' Christie was close to fainting when Albert moved sharply to send him away, from the trap into eternity.

Albert's last Yorkshire appointment was to despatch a soldier, Philip Henry, who had raped and murdered Flora Gilligan in York in March 1953. This was a particularly repulsive crime; the victim was seventy-six years of age. Henry, who was due to go on active service abroad the next day, was nailed by forensic work, some splinters of wood being found on him, and these matched the wood on the window frame at the house in Diamond Street, York, where the crime was committed. There was also a matching fingerprint found, so Henry had little hope of acquittal and indeed at the trial in York, after a request by the jury to visit the scene of crime, was found guilty of murder. Albert stepped into work at Armley, the place where Steve Wade normally worked, to hang Henry.

The Pierrepoint dynasty of hangmen undoubtedly created a great deal of professionalism and pride in their work. Albert is the one from the family whose career has had the most prominence in the media and in biography, and one aspect of that long career that needs to be stressed is that he withstood a huge amount of pressure in all kinds of contexts, from the war crimes work to his responses given to commissions on capital punishment. On top of that

DEBATE ON DEATH PENALTY

M.P.s' CALL FOR SUSPENSION

FIVE-YEAR EXPERIMENT PROPOSED

By Our Political Correspondent

Labour M.P.s have tabled 39 questions on foreign affairs to be answered by Sir Anthony Eden in the House of Commons to-day, and about half of these relate to various aspects of the Formosa crisis. In one question Mr. Bing will ask for the date upon which the United Kingdom Government considered they were no longer bound by the Cairo and Potsdam declarations on the future of Formosa, and the dates on which the decision was communicated to the other Governments which joined in the declaration.

Other questions will suggest the proposal to the Powers immediately interested of a pact of non-intervention in the Chinese civil war; and the refusal of facilities at Hong-kong for the repair or refuelling of any warships engaged in operations against the territory or forces of Communist China.

The principal debate of the week in the House of Commons will be that on capital

Debate on the death penalty, 1955. The Times

he had to carry on acting with 'restraint, discretion and self-respect' when the work he did was repeatedly questioned as attitudes changed. Certainly after the hanging of Ruth Ellis and then with the growing understanding that Timothy Evans had been hanged for a crime he did not commit (his wife having been killed by Christie) there was cause for self-examination and reflection. He had shown the Prison Commission that he could keep up the requirement to show 'complete reticence', as their handbook put it in the 1930s.

Albert's resignation came with a dispute about fees. After the execution of a man named Bancroft, in Manchester, Albert

Steve Wade. Laura Carter

wrote to the commissioners, after the man had been reprieved: 'On returning home I was only paid my out of pocket travelling expenses.' Then, nothing being settled to his satisfaction, he wrote on 23 February 1956: 'In the circumstances I have made up my mind to resign and this letter must be accepted as a letter of resignation. I request the removal of my name from the list of executioners forthwith.'

Albert died on 10 July 1992, in a nursing home. His former assistant, Steve Wade, had retired through ill-health in October 1955, just before Albert's last year in office. Just a year after Albert's resignation the 1957 Homicide Act, introduced by Sidney Silverman, passed in the Commons, but as Charles Duff put it in his book, *A Handbook on Hanging*, it got 'short shrift when it went to the House of Lords'; but there is a deep irony in the fact that hanging was 'suspended' for the whole of 1956.

CHAPTER 10

Steve Wade
(in office 1941–55)

I was incensed by the brutality of a crime when I was only twenty-one and I sent my name forward to the Home Office.

Steve Wade comes down to us from one photograph; our image of him is of a man with a drink and a cigarette, the face suggesting someone under pressure, maybe a nervous type. That is not associated with a hangman, of course. What the image does convey is that he was maybe ill when the picture was taken. He was not in office long – from 1941 to 1955 – and had to retire through ill health. He died in 1959, having been assistant to both Tom and Albert Pierrepoint. Steve handled twenty-nine hangings as chief executioner, and he had some really difficult cases.

He once said that he 'carried out more executions than I could remember' and that suggests a man who was not necessarily meticulous. He also pointed out that hanging was a sideline. Indeed it was, because he was in the transport business in Doncaster. If a full biography of him was ever written, the subtitle might read: 'Executioner and bus owner.' When he wrote to the Home Office to offer his services, he was at first refused as he was so young, but Wade must have been determined because he wrote again later and then was accepted. He was placed on a waiting list and given the usual course of instruction, before being appointed deputy to Thomas Pierrepoint.

Wade went to live in Doncaster in 1935 and he established his coaching business in the Waterdale area. He must have had a sense of humour (very dark) because, according to Brian

Bailey, Wade tricked Albert Pierrepoint into thinking that both he and Wade were needed to be at the post-mortem of a young man from Burma who had murdered his wife, after they had executed the man. The pathologist involved was the famous Keith Simpson. According to Molly Lefebure, who was Simpson's secretary at the time, Pierrepoint walked into the set-up scene and said: 'If you don't mind, I'd like to take a look at my handiwork.' That hardly seems in keeping with the man, and if he did, he would have seen a fracture dislocation between the second and third clavical vertebrae. Bailey makes the point that such a detail signifies the quickest and 'cleanest' death for a victim of the hangman's art.

Wade's first job as assistant was with Tom Pierrepoint at Wandsworth, where they hanged George Armstrong, a man who spied for Germany, starting that work after contacting a German consul in the USA. He was tried at the Old Bailey, then appealed and after that failed, found himself facing the noose. But before Steve Wade began his main work in Yorkshire, he had a job with Albert hanging another spy that turned out to be a terrible ordeal. Wade took a few notes on jobs, and this one on William Cooper at Bedford in 1940 is typical. Tom and Albert were the official hangmen, but Wade must have been there to observe and to learn because he recorded:

> William Henry Cooper at Bedford, aged 24. Height, five feet five and a half inches. Weight 136 lbs. Drop 8 feet one inch. Assisted to Scaffold. Hanged 9 a.m. on Nov. 26 1940.

He notes that the personnel present were 'Pierrepoint, Wade and Allen' but that does not tally with the official record.

As time went on he wrote more, as in the case of Mancini for which he noted: 'Three appeals with the House of Lords.' But the ordeal was to come with the execution of the spy, Karel Richter. Richter's records have now been released and we know that his mission was to deliver funds and a spare wireless crystal to another spy. He was given a code and money and also a supply of secret ink and was even briefed on what to say if interrogated. Acccording to some opinions, his arrival on espionage work was part of a 'double-cross' system which

Military staff accompany the spy Richter at his hide-out. Laura Carter

meant that agents were captured and given an option either to work as double agents or to face the gallows.

Richter was parachuted into Hertfordshire in 1941 and it appears that Churchill wanted him executed, as other agents had landed and not been hanged. That might be arguable, but what happened, according to MI5, is that Richter landed on the 14 May and that war reserve constable Boot, at London Colney, saw a lorry driver talking to a man who turned out to be the spy. Sergeant Palmer of St Albans was informed and came to assist. Richter was taken to Fleetville Police Station and there he showed a Czech passport. When searched he had a ration book, a compass, cash and a map of East Anglia.

Richter was seen by a girl, Florrie Cowley (nee Chapman) who recalls going to visit her divisional campsite, of the guides, at Colney Heath and that she and a friend went into a storage hut. There they saw evidence of very recent occupation. She wrote in a memoir: 'We quickly came out to think the situation over. Being war time there were no vagabonds or tramps etc. around so who could be living there? We then thought a German spy could have dropped ...' They were right. Photographs survive of Richter going back to the field with army and police to find his buried equipment. Richter stands in one photograph, pointing, while surrounded by personnel. He was destined to be Pierrepoint and Wade's client on 10 December 1941.

Wade kept notes on what happened that day. It was a horrendous experience for the young hangman, so early in his career. First he wrote: 'Karl Richter, 29, five feet and eleven and a half inches. 172 lbs. Execution: good under the circumstances.' That has to be one of the greatest understatements ever written. Richter was athletic, strong and determined to cause the maximum resistance when the hangmen arrived at the death cell. Wade wrote:

> On entering cell to take prisoner over and pinion him he made a bolt towards the door. I warded him off and he then charged the wall at a terrific force with his head. This made him most violent. We seized him and strapped his arms at rear . . . The belt was faulty, not enough eyelid holes, and he broke away from them. I shouted to Albert, 'He is loose!' and he was held by warders until we made him secure. He could not take it and charged again for the wall screaming HELP ME!

Things were still very difficult, as the man then had to be manhandled by several warders. Even at the scaffold, Richter fought:

> . . . he then tried to get to the opposite wall over the trap. Legs splayed. I drew them together and see Albert going to the lever. I shout wait, strap on legs and down he goes. As rope was fixed around his neck he shook his head and the safety ring, too big, slips . . .

Wade's notes have a tone of relief as he writes, finally: 'Neck broken immediately.' At the end of his notes he wrote that he said something to Albert, a comment along the lines of: 'I would not miss this for £50 . . .'

Richter actually stated under questioning that he had declined to take a part in the 'double cross system'. He had been a marine engineer and had a child in the USA. He was interned and returned to Germany after trying to return to America. In Germany he was recruited by the Abwehr (the German intelligence and counter intelligence organisation). Nigel West, in his history of MI5, has a coda to add to Steve Wade's terrible memoir:

> The grisly scene had a profound effect on all those present, and, indirectly, on some other Abwehr agents. Several months later Pierrepoint and his chief assistant, Steve Wade, carried out an execution at Mountjoy in Dublin. News of Richter's final moments reached Gunther Schutz and his fellow internees ... Irish warders gleefully recounted the details of the struggle on the scaffold, sending Richter's former colleagues into a deep depression.

In the war years, Wade was also on duty to hang a Canadian soldier who had committed a terrible murder of an old man in Halifax. Mervin McEwen was on the loose, camping out on the large area of Savile Park in Halifax when he befriended Mark Turner, aged eighty-two. Mr Turner lived on Moorfield Street, very close to the park, and he invited McEwen and another man to have a drink at his home. The soldier went back to his hut

Savile Park, Halifax. The author

Moorfield Street, where Turner was killed. The author

on the park after that, but Turner was found battered to death on his settee the next morning and McEwen was nowhere to be found. But the killer had been very careless: there were finger-prints found on a whisky bottle and also battledress and badges from McEwen's regiment, the Royal Canadian Corps. Not surprisingly, there was no sign of the killer. He had run away to Manchester and was about to start a new life with a new identity and a partner, a woman called Annie Perfect. He was then known as James Acton. He must have thought that he had a bolt-hole and was surely beyond being traced, but he was wrong.

Something happened that reinforces the view that steady, methodical police work pays dividends, and that even the craftiest villains fall foul of their own arrogance. The Canadian dropped his guard and did something so foolish, it seems amazing that he was caught so easily.

A constable arrived at his new house, simply making routine enquiries, but when he explained who he was, McEwen produced an identity card with the name Mark Turney on it. The officer was smart and suspicious, so he asked for a signature. He had seen that the letter 'r' had been changed to a 'y' and there was something amiss. The change had been done clumsily so it was easily noticed. Amazingly, McEwen signed as Mervin Turney. The game was up.

The killer saw that any attempt to lie his way out of the situation was futile and he gave himself up. His story was that he had indeed gone back to the old man's house in Halifax, cooked some food and drunk some whisky. In this state, he struck Turner as he woke up, claiming that it was not intentional. His main line of thought was that he was intoxicated and could not have planned murder. He failed, and in forty minutes, the jury at Leeds found him guilty of murder. Tom Pierrepoint and Wade hanged him at Armley on 3 February 1944.

From 1947, Wade did several hangings in Leeds, beginning with Albert Sabin from Morley, who murdered Dr Neil Macleod at Topcliffe Pit Lane in 1947. Sabin had been seen running and getting into the doctor's car in the early afternoon of 21 September, 1946. Sabin was just twenty-one, and in his army uniform. At around 2.30 pm that same day a shot was heard in the lane.

The doctor was found dead only a short time after his murder by Harry Philpott, as he was walking near to the Topcliffe pit. The scene was like one of Hitchcock's more macabre episodes, as poor Harry followed a trail of blood, then a knife and finally a gun. Then there was the body of MacLeod in a hollow, having been shot three times as it turned out.

The hunt was on for the doctor's car, a Ford V8. It was not a difficult task in those naïve days when occasional, opportunist criminals (unlike the professionals of course) merely took their victim's property and did not think too much about forward planning. Sabin was found in Pudsey, where his car was parked, and arrested. There was also no question of any mindgames or ploys to buy time and cause trouble: Sabin simply confessed to the killing when accosted.

The issue was whether or not this was a murder; but it was ascertained that Sabin took the gun with him when he went to meet the doctor, and that he had at least an intention to rob, and most likely to do grievous bodily harm if resisted. Taking the victim's life was merely one more step away from that, with a related intention of 'malice aforethought'. The only further complication came later when the killer tried to say that the doctor had made sexual advances to him; there were semen stains found on clothing, but they could have occurred just as naturally as part of the shock of death as much as in a sexual encounter, so nothing was conclusive there. Sabin claimed that on the day of the murder, Macleod had said he would give Sabin a lift back to camp, but then had driven to a place where he could make his advances. Naturally, Sabin tried to construct a narrative which culminated in a struggle and consequently that the gun had fired with no intention on Sabin's part to take life. That story did not convince the jury and Steve Wade, along with Harry Kirk, had a client at Armley – just twenty-one and a hardened killer – waiting for them in the death cell in January 1947.

The team of Wade and Kirk were busy in the summer of that year at Leeds. Wade and Kirk did three hangings by the end of 1949 and Wade had another assistant for yet another Leeds execution in that eighteen months. Wade's victims were from that area of life we might call domestic-tragic. Their killings were of women, either known to them or prostitutes. The men waiting for the noose at Armley were invariably killers driven by sexual passion, or aggression while drunk or, of course, a combination of all these. Typical was the case of the sad murder of Edith Simmonite in Sheffield. Edith spent a night enjoying a few drinks in the *Sun Inn* and she had been in company with two men who lived at a nearby hostel – William Smedley being one of them. On the night on which someone murdered Edith, Smedley's bed at West Bar had not been slept in. There were sound testimonies to that fact later.

So when Edith's body was found, strangled and after having sex, it was a case of basic police work to find out who she had been with and where she had spent her time that day. The task was made even more straightforward by the fact that she was known to the police as a local prostitute. When questioned, Smedley clearly relied on the man with him to back him up in a lie – that the two men had parted from the woman that night and seen her go into her room. Smedley's tale was not verified by his companion, and so the option open to him then was to invent another suspect. He did this by inventing 'an Irishman' who had ostensibly been in Edith's company. He even claimed that the mysterious Irishman had confessed to the murder to him (Smedley). Smedley had been interviewed twice, and told a plausible tale, so was released on both occasions.

What was also very disturbing and seedy about this case was that Edith's body was found by a young boy. Peter Johnson was out looking for wood in the old buildings in the areas of the city that had received bomb damage when he found the body. He said: 'I looked through the doorway and saw a woman lying face downwards at one end of the room. I ran and fetched Ronnie [his friend] . . . and then we went to tell a bus man.' Edith was only twenty-seven, and she also had been living in a women's hostel in the same West Bar area. Her hostel landlord had not seen her since the Friday, and her body was found on Sunday.

The man must have been at least partially convincing, because he claimed the killer had gone to Rhyl and the police gave Smedley the benefit of the doubt, going with him to Rhyl to try to find the killer. Nothing came of that. Not long after, Smedley told the truth to his sister.

The killer had one more story to tell in order to try to create some kind of desperate extenuating circumstances around the vicious murder. He said that he had had sex with Edith but then she had told him that she had a venereal disease, so this information prompted him to attack her, and he lost control in his rage.

None of this achieved anything that would save him from the scaffold; he was hanged by the Wade-Kirk duo in August 1947. Smedley had been told that he had no chance of an appeal, but in sheer desperation he tried the last ploy – a letter to the Home Secretary asking for a pardon. As Sheffield writer, David Bentley, has written in his book *The Sheffield Hanged*: 'The execution attracted no interest, not a single person being present when the statutory notices were posted outside.'

A hanging at Leeds in March 1950 was one of those cases that once again highlighted the complex moral and legal issues around the execution of young people. Two young men, Walter Sharpe and Gordon Lannen, robbed a jeweller's shop in Albion Street and the jeweller decided to fight them. In the struggle, Abraham Levine, forty-nine, was battered during this attempt to save his goods from being stolen by force. He was cracked with a gun butt and still would not let go his hold on one of the robbers. Then two shots were fired and Levine was mortally wounded.

Sharpe was twenty and Lannen only seventeen. They had some imaginative notions, perhaps from gangster films, because they fired their guns into the air as they ran away. Both had firearms and the most tragic footnote to the story is that they went away with no stolen goods at all. Their victim died the next day.

Simple ballistic analysis linked the bullets in Leeds to bullets fired at a robbery in Southport and the villains were tracked down. Under questioning, it emerged that Sharpe had fired the fatal shots. As in hundreds of similar cases, the defence was naturally that the gun went off in the struggle, and that defence failed. They had robbed before, while armed, and they had been reckless outside as well as in the premises.

In court matters were straightforward: as a crime was being committed, firearms were discharged. It was murder. Of course, that led to the inevitable conclusion: the elder man to be hanged and the younger, teenager, to be a guest of His Majesty for a very long time. Their choice of Albion Street, right at the very heart of the shopping centre of Leeds then as now, meant that they were firing guns in the vicinity of passers-by, citizens of all ages, going about their daily business.

But of course, the old discussions came back: there were only three years difference in the two young men, yet the older one was to hang. On the other hand, the older one had fired the gun that killed the victim. The 1908 Act had banned the execution of persons under sixteen, and in 1938 that age was raised to eighteen, after some high profile cases led to prolonged debate.

Walter Sharpe was hanged at Armley on 30 March 1950. Wade and Harry Allen officiated.

Towards the end of his short period in office, Wade had two victims both called Moore. The first, Alfred Moore, was found guilty of killing two police officers and so his story made all the papers and provoked those elements of society in favour of retaining the death penalty to insist that for the murder of police officers, hanging should always be the sentence. In the 1957 Homicide Act, there were five definite instances in which hanging should be applied and one was: 'Any murder of a police officer acting in the execution of his duty or of a person assisting a police officer so acting.' Moore's killing had done much to put that sentence there.

The double murder took place in the most unlikely of places: the quiet suburb of Huddersfeld, Kirkheaton, at Whinney Close Farm. Even today, this is an area in which older property with ample gardens stand side by side with newer suburban developments, quiet, occupied by families, and on the edge of the town, not far from the fields and smallholdings around Lepton.

In July 1951, Alfred Moore was a smallholder there, keeping poultry. But he also had a sideline in burglary to earn some extra cash. He was evidently not very skilled in his criminal activities and the police soon had him marked for observation. On 15 July the police surrounded his little homestead with the intention of catching him with stolen goods on him or on his property.

It was a stake-out that went badly wrong. In that very peaceful early morning of the Sunday, shots were fired in Kirkheaton and as officers moved around in the dark, trying to communicate and find the source of the gunfire, it was discovered that two officers had been shot: Duncan Fraser, a detective inspector, was found dead, and PC Jagger was severely wounded.

It was learned that Moore was holed up inside his house and it was inevitable that he would eventually be captured. The only glitch in the investigation was that, as a revolver had been used in the killings, a revolver had to be found on the person or the property and that never happened. Moore had a shotgun. But despite the use of a metal-detector, a revolver was never located.

But of course, PC Jagger was still alive so there was a witness to the dreadful events of that early morning. From his hospital bed, Jagger picked out Moore from a line-up. In a stunning piece of bravery and high drama, a specially formed court was formed at the hospital so that Jagger, almost certainly dying, could testify. Moore was tried for murder in Leeds; PC Jagger died just the day after giving evidence. Wade and Allen were busy at Armley once again.

The other Moore was a partner in a car sales company, along with Tom Bramley. They naturally met with other car dealers and one of these was Edward Watson. This terrible tale began with the sale of a faulty vehicle to Moore, sold by Watson at a cost of £55 (in 1954 a large sum). That transaction was to lead to a murder at the darkly fated area of Fewston, near the reservoir in Swaledale, where two more murders had occurred.

Fewston churchyard. The author

It was when the car was sold back to Watson at a loss that
trouble started brewing. Moore wanted to get his own back
after the dodgy deal. Moore arranged to meet and then drive his
enemy to Harrogate to see a vehicle. That was the black beginning of a brutal plan, because Moore had a rifle fitted with a
silencer for that journey. He had been careless, though, because
he had a spade in the back of his car and that was noticed by
others; later that would be very much against him.

Harrogate is only about eight miles from Fewston, along the
scenic road towards Blubberhouses (going along the dale finally
to Skipton) and in fact Moore had shot his victim five times and
then driven out to the desolate spot to bury him. Mrs Watson
was obviously worried about her husband's disappearance and
police questioned Moore, who claimed that Watson had never
turned up for their meeting and jaunt to Harrogate. People
knew about both the rifle and the spade, and an officer called
Wilby persisted with his questioning of the dealer.

The killer boldly said to the officer: 'You don't think I've shot
and killed him do you?'

That was a neat summary of the actual events. Moore grew
desperate and he actually tried to take his own life, but then he
caved in and confessed, beginning to formulate a tall tale about
a fight with the gun and an accidental death. There were lots of
anomalies in statements made – things that did not sit easily
with the forensic evidence. In court, it became clear that this
was a case of murder and Moore was sentenced to hang.

Wade's last hanging was a more mundane case: simply a man
killing his wife's mother – the woman who had stood in the
way, as he saw it, of his happiness with Maureen Farrell of
Wombwell. Her mother, Clara, became an object of hatred for
the young man, Alec Wilkinson, only twenty-two years old. On
1 May 1955, Wilkinson had a great deal to drink and worked
himself up to a mood of extreme violence and enmity towards
Clara Farrell.

Not long after their marriage, Alec and Maureen had been
under pressure, and the relationship between Alec and his
mother-in-law was one of extreme emotional tension, she
apparently always criticising him and making it clear that he

was worthless (at least that is how he claimed to see the situation). On the fateful day when he walked up to the front door of the Farrell's home in Wombwell, he had a burning spite in him and he was in a mood to use it. First he sprang on Clara and punched her and then slammed her head on the floor.

But such was the man's fury that he went for a knife in the kitchen, stabbed her, and then did something that suggests a psychosis as well as a drunken fit: he piled furniture on the woman and set fire to it. Wilkinson left as someone came to try to put out the fire, but later Alec confessed and one of his statements was that he was not sorry for what he had done. There was an attempt to demonstrate provocation, and even a petition top save him, but Wilkinson was found guilty of murder at Sheffield and sentenced to hang. This time, on Wade's last appearance as hangman, when he was becoming too ill to do any more, his assistant was Robert Stewart.

Steve Wade returned to Doncaster and lived on Thorne Road, Edenthorpe. He had been a café proprietor and he operated Wade's Motor Coaches. He retired in 1955 and died on 22 December 1956, at Doncaster Royal Infirmary – just over a year after hanging Wilkinson. The only teasing question about his official obituary is this note: 'Buried at Rosehill Cemetery (unconsecrated) in Doncaster.' He seems to have been a very reticent character. Syd Dernley, who worked with him, said simply: 'Wade was a quiet man and said no more than hello when Kirky did the introductions.'

Perhaps the laconic Albert Pierrepoint said the simplest and best thing about Steve Wade, in his autobiography, *Executioner: Pierrepoint*, when being questioned about his work. He was asked: 'Do you know whether any of those who are at present on the list [the official Home Office list of hangmen] have ever carried out an execution?'

Pierrepoint replied: 'Only one, and he has done five or six. Steve Wade, a good, reliable man.'

Part Two

Obscure Figures and Dark Tales

CHAPTER 11

Some Assistants

The first hanging was shattering. As a trainee executioner I was there to watch. I did not have to do anything except stay on my feet and keep my breakfast down ... (Syd Dernley)

All the chief executioners began as assistants after the turn of the nineteenth century. Before that it had been a case of learning by doing. Marwood was unusual, practising drops with sacks in his home village of Horncastle. Others before the more organised years would not be too concerned about standards and wanted the pay, and of course plenty of drink to steel them to the task in hand.

In the twentieth century it became essential for a new man on the Home Office list to learn by observation and to be properly instructed in all the elements of the job, including appropriate behaviour and tact. We do not have many memoirs of hangmen generally and some of those in print are not very helpful. John Ellis did talk to a 'ghost writer' and there are books by Pierrepoint and by Dernley. But the other assistants are shadowy figures. We sometimes have just a few bare facts about them. The main web site source for hangmen lists twenty-one men who worked as assistants in the twentieth century. Of these, four worked in Yorkshire from time to time, but undoubtedly Dernley and Allen have the most interest in terms of Yorkshire-based cases. In the late Victorian period, Thomas Henry Scott of Moldgreen, Huddersfield was on the list from 1892 to 1901 and at times was the main executioner. We know that Scott assisted Berry but little else has come down to us. There is one anecdote of Scott, though. When he was working in Ireland (in Londonderry) he was the target of a wild mob who threw rotten vegetables at him as he travelled in a cab to the prison. It seems he was also robbed on one occasion in Liverpool; Steve Fielding tells the tale:

> On arriving at Lime Street Station, he shared a taxi with a young woman of questionable virtue, Winifred Webb, and instead of heading directly for the gaol they chose to cruise around the city for a while. On reaching his destination and after bidding farewell to his companion, Scott discovered that he had been robbed of £2-9s-6d and a pair of spectacles.

When Scott stepped into the police station to report that, there was the woman, claiming she had been robbed; she was arrested and, of course, it was embarrassing for the hangman, who should have stuck to routine and gone straight to Walton Gaol.

Syd Dernley (in office: 1949–54)

Dernley wrote a chatty, darkly humorous autobiography of his life as a hangman, from his first interview in Lincoln to his last memories of working with the more famous characters. In later life he showed a macabre interest in the trappings of his trade and was only too pleased to regale the media with his tales.

When Dernley was interviewed in 1994 he was happy to pose for the camera with his ropes dangled in front of him. It was noted then that he had been in office from 1949 to 1954 and that he was 'never given an official reason' for that removal. Syd was from North Nottinghamshire, living in Mansfield when interviewed, and he was patently pleased to show off his equipment and mementos to the interviewer. He displayed his case, with a hood inside, a legstrap, armstrap and a replica noose. The interviewer noted that Syd enjoyed 'gallows humour'.

Syd Dernley, hangman. Laura Carter

Dernley even used to have a full-size working gallows when he ran a shop in Mansfield, taken from a prison in Liverpool; he noted that he had to sell them. He gave a similar reason to Harry Pierrepoint when asked why he had done the work: 'It was not that I wanted to kill people, but it was the story of travel and adventure, of seeing notorious criminals and meeting famous detectives.' But the usual moral complexities arose in the interview when he was asked about the hanging of Timothy Evans, clearly as it turned out, innocent of the murder of his wife. Dernley said: 'Well, if I helped to kill an innocent man as you seem to be implying, it doesn't worry me one little bit. I did the job I was trained to do, and I did it well.'

Dernley's most interesting Yorkshire connection was, oddly, with a man hanged at Strangeways. Nicholas Crosby had killed Ruth Massey at Springfield Road, Leeds, in July 1950. He had cut her throat after taking her home following a night drinking in the *Brougham Arms*.

Crosby had given a story of what he had done to his sister, confessing to the murder, but then changed the tale for the police. He claimed that there had been another man and that he heard a scream after walking away, leaving Ruth and the stranger together. His reply to a direct question about whether he killed the woman or not was: 'To be sure sir, I don't know if I did . . . if I did, I don't remember.' He was found guilty of murder and because some execution chambers were being modernised at Armley, Crosby was sent to Strangeways to die. Dernley described the man: 'Crosby was a twenty-two-year-old gypsy . . . he was to give any number of versions as to what happened.'

Dernley worked with Albert Pierrepoint for the job. What became remarkable about this was that, as Dernley recalled, a man came along to Pierrepoint's Manchester pub, *Help the Poor Struggler* with the intention of bribing the hangmen so he could get a picture of a hanging. The man said: 'Look, I've got a business proposition to make to you.' He wanted to get a camera into the whole process.

When Dernley told him it was impossible, the man said: 'No, it's not, we will supply you with a miniature camera, a tiny thing. It's so small you'll be able to wear it on your shirt and it'll

be hidden behind your tie until the moment he goes down . . .'
Of course, Dernley refused.

One thing we have from Syd Dernley is detailed accounts of
the events at his executions. In Crosby's case, he writes well of
such things, as in his account of entering the death cell: 'As it
turned out, we were right to be worried about Crosby. He was
scared out of his wits and when we entered the condemned cell
I think he came very, very close to breakdown and hysteria . . .'
The killer asked for the straps not to be tied too tightly, so
Dernley and Albert made sure that there were warders ready to
intervene if anything devious was planned. As Dernley wrote:
'Crosby was down and dead in a split second.' He then notes
that two assistants had come along to watch and learn –
Doncaster man Harry Smith and Robert Stewart. Dernley
commented: ' . . . poor Smith and Stewart! In the corridor they
must have heard all the commotion without being able to see
what the hell was going on. One look at their faces was enough
to tell that it had been quite unnerving . . . not a good job for
their first experience of executions.'

Dernley's other Yorkshire tale involves the Hull killer, James
Inglis. Inglis is the man who has gone down in the history
of hanging as the man who ran to the gallows. Like Crosby,
Inglis was hanged in Manchester, in May 1951. This tragic but
farcical story from court to gallows began when, being asked by
the judge if he had anything to say, Inglis said: 'I've had a fair
trial from you and the members of your court. All I ask now is
that you get me hanged as soon as possible.'

Inglis had been in the army, but there were deep personality
problems with him; he had a spell in a mental home before
coming to Hull, working in Hessle. He enjoyed his food and
he wanted sex from prostitutes. He met Alice Morgan, the
daughter of a skipper who had been married but divorced; when
she met Inglis she was living near the centre of Hull by the
railway station. They went out together for a while and then
one day he handed in his notice – one minute's notice – at his
work. He spent the day after that drinking with Alice, and they
quarrelled over money. When she said that she could earn an
easy £5 from any man that night, Inglis snapped and brutally
beat her up.

West Parade, Hull, close to Inglis's home. The author

The postman, Alfred Brougham, came to deliver a parcel at Alice's house in Cambridge Street and there was Alice's body on the sofa. She had been beaten on the face and strangled by a silk stocking. Inglis had already attacked a woman – his previous landlady, Amy Gray. He was therefore easy to trace, and he had been seen by a number of people in Alice's company. His story was that he lost his temper, hit Alice and then: 'The next thing I knew, she was dead.' Dernley relates what happened as the police went in search of Inglis:

> At the end, Inglis was pathetic and grovelling. They ran him to ground at Victoria Mansions, the Salvatian Army hostel for homelss down-and-outs in Great Passage Street, a stone's throw from Cambridge Street. He blurted out a confession as soon as Detective Inspector James Cocksworth identified himself.

There was a reasonable possibility that there could have been a defence of insanity at the trial in Leeds before Mr Justice Ormerod. He had said when arrested that he had gone 'mad' at two places (referring to Amy Gray). In his background there were certain details that might have helped to construct a defence: his maternal grandmother had suffered from insanity and died in a mental home and Inglis's discharge from the army had been ostensibly because of a personality disorder. But there was nothing in that material to persuade the jury that he had not intended to kill Alice Morgan and he must hang.

Dernley has left a detailed account of the man who ran to the gallows; he noted that Inglis in the death cell was playing cards with warders and that he had lost a lot of weight. Albert Pierrepoint was in charge and he knew immediately that Inglis was around 139 lb and a drop of eight feet would be needed (Dernley noted that was the longest he had ever seen).

Strangely, this bizarre execution was an event chosen for observation by the High Sheriff of Yorkshire. Both hangmen thought that such a visit was very rare and could not explain why it had happened. It was a foreboding for the strangeness to come. After they had eaten breakfast, the two hangmen went to the condemned cell and there was Inglis, smiling at them.

Inglis then turned and raised his hands behind him, ready for them to pinion him; he had done his homework on hanging procedure, it seemed. As Dernley commented: 'He was being so bloody helpful, he was getting in the way.' Then, as the door was open and he saw the waiting rope, Inglis moved out, ahead of the hangmen. Dernley wrote: 'The man was almost treading on Pierrepoint's heels to in his anxiety to get onto the gallows.' He wrote also that the group 'trotted' to the scaffold – a rare event indeed. The High Sheriff must have had a very odd impression of executions.

Dernley was sure that the death of Inglis was the fastest hanging on record, anywhere.

Harry Allen (in office 1950s to 1961)

Allen assisted Wade at the hanging of Alfred Moore, the police killer. He also was involved in the hanging of William Lubina at Leeds in 1954; Lubina was a Polish miner who had lodged with a couple called Ball at Springfield Street, Barnsley. He had developed a desire for the wife, Charlotte, and it emerged later that he had written to her expressing his feelings and that he was rejected. She had supposedly hit him at one point.

He lost all control on 25 June and, attacking Charlotte Ball in her home, he stabbed her several times and then ran in a frenzy to another room where he cracked his head repeatedly on a mirror. He had collected a stack of photos of his 'beloved' and clearly had a deep, twisted and unrequited love for her that was in the end a destructive, sick inversion of feelings of any kind of affection.

He had sharpened a knife at work before going to the Ball house that day so there was no doubt that the killing was planned. He was to hang, and Wade and Allen saw him off the scaffold to his death on 27 January, 1954.

Allen was a dapper, lively man with flair and style. We have a vivid account of him from ex-prison officer turned writer, Robert Douglas, who was on duty when Allen went to hang Russell Pascoe at Bristol in 1963. We learn much about Allen from a posed photograph of him, taken as he stands by a Rolls Royce, a tall man with overcoat, bowler hat and brolly – every inch the ex-army gentleman. Douglas wrote of the hangman:

'Allen is gregarious company. A tall, slim man in his late fifties, his hair short, clipped moustache and smart blue suit give him an almost distinguished air. He is a publican in Manchester. For around fifty years he has been number two to the doyen of British hangmen, Pierrepoint.'

Douglas recalled that Allen, on the night before the hanging, 'held the floor and regaled us with some of the jobs he and Pierrepoint had carried out over the years'.

Douglas's final note about Allen is that he returned just four minutes after pulling the lever to the officers' mess and picked up the cigarette he had left in the ashtray. He was asked if the man was any bother?

'Good as gold,' said Allen.

Allen also hanged the last man to die in Armley – the Hungarian Zsiga Pankotia. That was surely an example of the most clumsy, transparent and thick-headed killing on record, because all Pankotia had done was go to the home of pools winning market trader Eli Myers. Myers had made the mistake

of telling people that he had won the money – well over £1,000
– and so invited trouble.

Pankotia went to Myers' home in Street Lane to rob him,
but the trader confronted him. Pankotia picked up a breadknife
and the two had a long and desperate fight. In that struggle,
Myers was fatally wounded. Pankotia ran away, taking the
trader's van. He was soon tracked down and arrested, but the
real interest in this case was not in the banal and clumsy killing
but in the courtroom.

The famous forensic scientist from Leeds University, Pro-
fessor Poulson, made a statement that Myers had been suffering
from a heart complaint. Could he have died as a result of that
illness, rather than from the wounds inflicted in the struggle?
But that detail was not enough in the end. The jury thought that
the killing had happened 'in the furtherance of theft; the act of
1861, laying down the concept of grievous bodily harm applied
yet again: such an intent was also murderous and in this case
happened during a robbery. Pankotia had to hang.

There had to be some kind of lingering belief that the death
could have been from natural causes, however, as the case went
to the court of appeal, but no unsafe conviction was stated and
the first ruling was confirmed.

On the 29 June 1961 the gallows at Armley Gaol were used
for the last time and Harry Allen, with Harry Robinson, were
the last hangmen to work there.

Harry Smith (in office 1950s)

We know practically nothing about this Doncaster hangman
who assisted on various occasions, but we know for sure that he
was working with Steve Wade on the hanging of the man responsible for one of the worst, most heinous Halifax killings of
the twentieth century: the murder of little Mary Hackett, just
six years old, by Albert George Hall, caretaker of the Congregational Church in Lister Lane, Halifax. This was in August
1953, and the search for the missing girl had been the main
story in the Yorkshire papers during the days in which the
search for Mary grew increasingly desperate. The area around
the church was then one of old Victorian villas and wide, leafy
lanes. Mary went missing there after going out to play and after

The Congregational chapel where Hall worked. The author

twelve days, Scotland Yard were called in, and even blood-hounds from Wakefield.

In the end, the case was cracked by old-fashioned Holmesian observation. Hall, as caretaker in the church, had used his cunning to bury Mary's body beneath the crypt and placed under furniture and two opened tins of paint. Superintendent Ball noticed the opened tins and after some time he realised that they were open in all probability to cover another smell. Police began digging down to the crypt under the furniture and there they found little Mary's body. She had been brutally beaten in the face.

There was no evidence directly to convict Hall, but he was watched closely and later he went to a mental asylum where he had once been a patient. The police went to interview the doctor there (it was at Scalebor Park Hospital) and they learned that Hall had given information to the doctor that only the killer of Mary Hackett would have known.

Albert George Hall was tried at Leeds, and of course, with the mental health record being quite solid and documented, it was a difficult case. But after several hours of deliberation, the jury found Hall guilty of murder. Hall appealed, but that failed. Hall simply said to the judge: 'My Lord, I am not guilty of this.'

Lister Lane. The author

It did him no good, and he was in the hands of Smith and Wade on 22 April, to be marched to the scaffold and be sent to his death.

In February the next year, the principal debate in the House of Commons was that on the abolition of capital punishment. *The Times* reported:

The government will submit a motion asking the House to take note of the report of the Royal Commission under the chairmanship of Sir Earnest Gowers. No issue is raised by the Government motion, but the abolitionists will seize the opportunity of trying to persuade the House once more to declare itself in favour of the suspension of capital punishment for an experimental period of five years.

It came in the end, but for one year only. The hangmen, chiefs and assistants, must have thought their incomes and duties under threat of being no longer in demand. The old argument, expressed by John Ellis in interview: 'Hanging is clean. It's the cleanest way of them all for putting them away,' was being challenged more widely.

John Ellis, hangman. Laura Carter

CHAPTER 12

Some Tales of Bad Workmanship

It is only fair to the art of hanging to mention these bunglings and miscalculations. (Charles Duff)

Charles Duff, a barrister and linguist with an interest in crime history, wrote a little book in 1928 called *A Handbook on Hanging*. It was intended to be a wry, satirical account of the 'art of hanging' mainly in British history. The book was reprinted recently and to readers in a culture with no capital punishment, the satire is still there, but we have to reach further and try harder to understand the full implications of Duff's targets. This is important because, as there has not been a capital offence on our statute books since 1999, when the European Convention on Human Rights was applied to Britain's last such crimes, and also that no-one has been hanged in England since 1964, reading about hangings today is very different from 1928.

Duff's readers read about bunglings and errors that are painful to contemplate, and people before 1964 were fully aware that men and women were being hanged in several cities across the land. Discussion over the breakfast table might have been cut short to cater for the sensibilities of children when Duff wrote, but the media were always ready to come down hard on any issue related to capital punishment. One of the 'hottest' events was when a hanging went wrong and the scandal somehow reached the journalists:

Things that could go wrong ... consider the various elements of the hangman's art – every one of these tasks or features of the neck-stretching process could go wrong:

SCALE SHOWING THE STRIKING FORCE OF FALLING BODIES AT DIFFERENT DISTANCES.												
Distance Falling in Feet from Zero	8 Stone	9 Stone	10 Stone	11 Stone	12 Stone	13 Stone	14 Stone	15 Stone	16 Stone	17 Stone	18 Stone	19 Stone
	Cw. Qr. lb.	Cw Qr. lb.	Cw. Qr. lb.	Cw. Qr. lb.	Cw. Qr. lb.	Cw. Qr. lb.	Cw. Qr. lb.	Cw. Qr. lb.	Cw. Qr. lb.	Cw. Qr. lb.	Cw. Qr. lb.	Cw. Qr. lb.
1 Ft.	8 0 0	9 0 0	10 0 0	11 0 0	12 0 0	13 0 0	14 0 0	15 0 0	16 0 0	17 0 0	18 0 0	19 0 0
2 „	11 1 15	12 2 23	14 0 14	15 2 4	16 3 22	18 1 12	19 3 2	21 0 21	22 2 11	24 0 1	25 1 19	26 3 9
3 „	13 3 16	15 2 15	17 1 14	19 0 12	20 3 11	22 2 9	24 1 8	26 0 7	27 3 5	29 2 4	31 1 2	33 0 1
4 „	16 0 0	18 0 0	20 0 0	22 0 0	24 0 0	26 0 0	28 0 0	30 0 0	32 0 0	34 0 0	36 0 0	40 0 0
5 „	17 2 11	19 3 5	22 0 0	24 0 22	26 1 16	28 2 11	30 3 5	33 0 0	35 0 22	37 0 16	39 2 11	41 3 15
6 „	19 2 11	22 0 5	24 2 0	26 3 22	29 1 16	31 3 11	34 1 5	36 3 0	39 0 22	41 2 16	44 0 11	46 2 5
7 „	21 0 22	23 3 11	26 2 0	29 0 16	31 3 5	34 1 22	37 0 11	39 3 0	42 1 16	45 0 5	47 2 22	50 1 11
8 „	22 2 22	25 2 4	28 1 14	31 0 23	34 0 5	36 3 15	39 2 25	42 2 7	45 1 16	48 0 26	51 0 8	53 3 18
9 „	24 0 11	27 0 12	30 0 14	33 0 23	36 0 16	39 0 18	42 0 19	45 0 21	48 0 22	51 0 23	54 0 25	57 0 26
10 „	25 1 5	28 1 23	31 2 14	34 3 4	37 3 22	41 0 12	44 1 2	47 1 21	50 2 11	53 3 1	56 3 19	60 0 9

James Berry's 'Table of Drops', 1885. Author's collection

the lever might not work; someone else might stand on the trap; the rope might be weak; the metal eye might not tighten on the rope; a pinion might go loose; and the calculation of the drop might be wrong.

What could go wrong with the hangman ... the hangman was always under strain. Even the most superficially cool and professional was seething inside. Every judicial hanging was inescapably a judicial murder under another name, and the executioners perhaps knew that. But these were the factors involved that might be said to be a version of Sod's Law, perhaps better rephrased for the present purposes as 'Jack Ketch's Law': he might have had too much Dutch Courage; he might suffer from nerves; he might be affected by the victim's grovelling pleas for mercy; he might really feel that his client is innocent; he might think that another member of the team might be under par and therefore a liability; and he might suffer from the effects of pressures from the media of from superiors.

James Berry is arguably the name from the Yorkshire hangmen whose name is most readily associated with mistakes at the scaffold. Duff referred to him as the man who was respon-

Where Jack Ketch worked. Author's collection

sible for the 'Goodale mess'. This was a hanging in Norwich in 1885 of Robert Goodale, who had murdered his wife, Bathsheba, near Wisbech. What became know as The Walsoken Tragedy was the horrible tale of Goodale battering his wife, then hatcheting her, and throwing her body down a well. Clearly, there would be no plea for manslaughter. But he might have been considered insane. However, he was found guilty of murder and Berry travelled to Norwich to see him from this life.

There was a certain aspect of foreboding in the Goodale case; a prison warder, on Berry's arrival, said that he had had a dream that something was going to go wrong. There was widespread gossip and warning talk about Goodale's difficult personality. He was said to be an awful coward and that there would be trouble in the death cell.

Goodale was a large man, almost six feet tall and very heavy. Berry had his own table of drops and had worked out a drop but then reduced it by two feet, for reasons that are not clear. This big man was to drop five feet nine inches to his death. To make things worse, the condemned man had pleaded his cause to the governor and there had been a last-ditch deputation to the Home Office. But when the end was determined, the most important thing was to test the workings of the trap and use weights. This was done twice, and everything was in working order.

In this fretful atmosphere, Berry went to see his victim in the death cell, but did not let the man know that Berry was the hangman. Later hangmen made a special point of doing this on occasions when there was a degree of tact and delicacy involved, rather than merely observing the condemned through a small slot in the door.

Berry in his memoirs, described what happened: it was a tough ordeal for Berry and all the officials, because the man screamed like an animal, whimpered and raged, to such an

James Berry, hangman. Author's collection

James Berry · PUBLIC EXECUTIONER from 1884 to 1892

extent that he aroused and excited all the other convicts. To make things worse, there was a large crowd outside: 'Peeping from the opening in the doorway the warder on duty could see that consternation had seized the crowd when they realised that it was a long way past the time for the execution . . .'

Then Berry began to waiver; he wrote: 'I was trembling myself and wishing it were all over.' He could not tie the straps, so a warder went to get some wire. Then the little group started to move along to the scaffold, but Goodale stood firm like a child refusing to cooperate. Berry's description of Goodale explains why the case was so horrifying: 'His eyes were staring wildly, his face was ashen with terror, and his huge body was quivering to and fro.'

The man was dragged to the noose by a whole gang of warders. On the trap, Goodale screamed for forgiveness from God and fell to the ground. The warders had to keep hold of Goodale or all could go wrong – and the worst happened. The victim went down, but so did a warder. Berry noted that: 'He was clutching the sides of the opening and it was only by the mercy of providence that he did not crash down to the foot of the well.'

The worst aspect of this sad case was that Goodale had been decapitated.

William Calcraft, the Victorian hangman before Berry and Marwood, was a proud man and he had a very high profile status in Victorian society. But he had his bunglings too. The antics of John Wiggins on the scaffold in 1867 show this inept side to Calcraft. Wiggins was a powerful young man and he fought hard, after realising that the straps tied by Calcraft were not as firm as they should have been. After four burly warders had grabbed the villain, Calcraft could not get the white cap on and Wiggins yelled that he was innocent but that he would rather have his head cut off than be hanged.

Even Marwood had his lapses. At Durham he had to hang a man called Brownless and things went wrong: as one witness wrote:

On looking down into the pit where the body hung we observed that the feet were about within half an inch off the ground; the rope, which was about an inch and a half thick, was embedded in the neck and blood was slowly trickling down the breast.

It was said of Calcraft, who did his work in all areas of the land, including Yorkshire, but we have few records, that he was more afraid of the crowds at hangings than the condemned convicts were. This is one of the signs of the demise of the hangman – the loss of nerve that almost always descended like a black cloud on them. After the end of public executions in 1868 much of the most horrible material that may have come down to historians was lost. Unless the executioner in question kept a logbook and then wrote memoirs, evidence of bungled jobs was always hard to come by. In Calcraft's last phase in office, his mess in the case of James Connor was arguably his least successful work. When Calcraft pulled the lever, he rope pinioning Connor in position then snapped. Connor was in agony on the floor, but not dropping to his doom. It took a second attempt to achieve that.

Of course, in some slight defence of the Yorkshire hangman with the worst reputation for botched work, it is only fair to mention one of Thomas Askern's most efficient hangings. It was a melancholy affair, as the victim, Charles Normington, from Leeds, was only eighteen. He had attacked and killed a man called Broughton who had taken a long walk from Roundhay towards the town centre. The young man had submitted to the law and to the whole process towards the scaffold, and though he was illiterate, he dictated letters stating that he was content that he had had an impartial trial and that he was at peace and resigned to his doom.

Askern, as *The Times* reported, did a good job: 'The convict calmly submitted to his fate, and died after a few convulsive struggles after the bolt had been drawn. The last words he was heard to say were: 'The Lord have mercy upon my soul.' The executioner was a man named Askern, of Maltby, near Rotherham, who has before discharged similar painful duties near York.'

Around 7,000 people saw Normington hang, and we have to note that phrase, ' he died after a few convulsive struggles'.

The date was 1860 – many years after the worst excesses of the amateur convicts-turned-hangmen who plied that trade. Spin the report one way and we have a successful hanging; spin it another way and we have an implication that the young man spent perhaps a few (very long) minutes in agony because Askern had no knowledge of the sub-mandible position by the carotid artery where a more humane man would have placed the knot. William Marwood's entrance into the hangman's trade was only another fifteen years after that. In short, every-thing is relative: in comparison to the common eighteenth century Newgate roughness of the hangings at Tyburn, when relatives often had to pull on their dying relatives' legs to ensure a quick death, Askern had perhaps done 'a good job'.

What bungled executions highlight is that delicate, difficult subject of the hangman-client interchange. Such a meeting can hardly be called a 'relationship' but the few days of process, observation, preparation and hanging do contain a number of elements which show the aspects of the hangman's work that have not perhaps been duly credited: the care and consideration required to give the convict a speedy death, and also a death that has as little pain and shock as possible. In later days, when the art of the quick death was a matter of professional pride, it seems that the hangmen were only too glad to let the public know that they had been so humane (as well as efficient). That tends to eclipse the demeaning phrase of 'the public hangman' – words so easily applied to a job which so few people are actually able to do.

Robert Douglas's account of Harry Allen despatching his client in between the smoking of a cigarette, together with the stunning ability the hangmen had to do such things and then engage in humorous anecdotes, are details indicating the neces-sary *sang-froid* needed. That quality is something not on the curriculum in the training. We note that the governors observed the trainee hangmen and paid as much attention to 'nerve' and demeanour as they did to the terrible mechanics of killing for the law. Most of the hangmen in England were people of certain indefinable qualities, but those surface features almost always hid a deeper, more tense reaction to the nasty work they were paid to do.

Their relatives mostly knew that the hangmen did that work, of course, but it was usually rarely on the agenda when it came to family conversation. Leonora Klein, biographer of Albert Pierrepoint, makes it clear that the hangmen's partners carried a terrible burden too; she writes of Mrs Pierrepoint: 'Anne married Pierrepoint in 1943; it is possible – just – to believe that she made do with dignified silence at the beginning. But Pierrepoint worked as an executioner for thirteen years after they were married and in that time he hanged more than 350 people. What did she do with all those ghosts?'

Taking a longer historical view, it is a lamentable thought that we know so little of the private lives of the early hangmen. But we can be sure that every era has its expressions of how it valued human life, and so large a stretch of English history gives evidence of human life being held at no more value than a bent sou that through modern eyes, the beliefs and justifications various hangmen had to explain their dark profession can only be guessed at with reference to other deaths and killings in their time.

When Askern was at work, for instance, the Crimean War was claiming thousands of lives (many deaths through illness, not the sword or bullet) and in the years of the Napoleonic Wars, several women were hanged at York. Life was cheap and the legal system all unchangeably black and white. Transgressions, in the days before the huge number of capital offences was reduced. Only rare individuals like John Howard, the prison reformer, could try to take time and trouble to change the system. Hangmen, being either convicts or members of

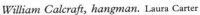

William Calcraft, hangman. Laura Carter

Dodd delin.   Page sculp.

A PIRATE *hanged at Execution Dock.*

A hanging showing a figure beneath ready to pull the legs of the victim. Author's collection

The everyday side of the Pierrepoints: Huddersfield gasworks, where Tom worked.
Author's collection

a desperately poor and ill-educated class, put money before morals.

In the end, the hangman's trade was attractive to a particular group of men with unsavoury and perhaps vicariously cruel natures and the state was in need of people who could either handle the massive and noisy popular hanging-day frenzies: whether they could do that through vanity or through Sadism was hardly an issue.

Following that was a long-standing morbid fascination with the hangmen, and most of these courted the popularity: James Berry had his business card decorated with delicate blossoms and Calcraft posed for the artist and camera in such a way that he looks like a famous statesman. The Yorkshire hangmen were characters who liked the limelight and welcomed the cash; they were mostly convivial and had difficulties in following the code of discretion and restraint the job entailed. But this history has shown that, in the twentieth century, they were largely successful in coping with that growth of the more questionable fascination with the materiality of death that has come with a mass-media soaked society.

Conclusions

The 1957 Homicide Act attempted to cope with one of the cornerstones of the concept and definition of murder: the idea of implied malice. A large element of this problem the experts had to discuss came from the problems and debates associated with the hanging of Derek Bentley. In the Act, this clause pinpoints the thinking about 'implied malice':

> . . . where a person kills another in the course or further-ance of some other offence, the killing shall not amount to murder unless done with the same malice aforethought (expressed or implied) as is required for a killing to amount to murder when not done in the course or furtherance of another offence.

This was to add to the drama of the murder trial and the court of appeal in that last seven years of capital punishment in England. This was because of the difficulty in ascertaining intention, of course, and that tough legal issue was partly so prominent in the media at the time because high-profile and morally repugnant hangings had taken place (notably the hang-ing of Ruth Ellis by Albert Pierrepoint in 1955). The hang-man had been a factor in a major legal debate in the criminal justice system. That could do nothing but add to the already significant celebrity of the executioners.

Some of that celebrity has naturally been created by the mystique of the trade and its arcane knowledge and procedures. But the process of judicial hanging in all its repulsive but intriguing detail is now available for all, on the internet as well as in memoirs. Again, the turning point in the specification of these duties and requirements was in the inter-war years. The Home Office issued directions on setting the drop, and on how the 'execution box' had the equipment ready and checked. The directions are in objective, cold language, such as: 'Take a piece of copper wire from Execution Box B, secure one end over the shackle on the end of the chain, and bend up the other end to coincide with the mark showing the drop.' After Marwood's first steps in such precision, it was Yorkshireman James Berry who used a particular table of drops. The reason why this detail is so important is that, although when a body drops from the scaffold down to a depth of drop of around five or six feet, the force exerted is so strong that profound damage is done to the corpse but the asphyxia actually extinguishing life is not applied any quicker. Therefore, for reasons of both humane killing and of the nature of the corpse when handled after death, the drop calculations need to be exact, but other preparations have to be perfect too.

James Berry, for all his occasional lapses, did show an impressive professionalism on most occasions. His notes on the techniques and considerations for the hanging procedure are meticulous and informative. He wrote on the drop, the rope, pinioning straps and scaffold, as well as explaining what he called 'the proceedings'. In the case of the latter, of course, many aspects of the proceedings – from death cell to scaffold – his words define much that had gathered mythic narrative status over the years. He wrote: 'In the carrying out of the last penalty of the law everything is conducted with decorum and solemnity, and so far as I can see there is no way in which the arrangements at an execution can be improved . . .'

Berry was aware that the ritual and the jealous guarding of the nature of events at private hangings tended to create these myths and fold tales, as he writes in the same notes: 'I know that there is a large section of the public that thinks the exclusion of the reporters must mean that there is something going on which there is a desire to hush up.' He simply adds that the public need to know, at the very least, that everything in those solemn events is carried out 'decently and in order.'

Since the abolition of hanging in 1964, the subject of hangmen has receded into one of those streams of social history that force us to revisit our past values and the long road towards enlightenment and humane attitudes in the moral arena of retribution and punishment. The lives of hangmen are therefore now partly an aspect of that new kind of documentary our society so much needs, the morbid curiosity about work and occupations involving repulsive and unwholesome tasks – jobs such as undertakers and sewage workers. This is to be lamented, because the work of hangmen in our history has been highly significant in all kinds of cultural contexts, from popular print genres such as *The Newgate Calendar* and *The Police News* to the more recent true crime television documentary.

Yorkshire, for reasons we may only theorise about and guess, has produced more than its fair share of hangmen. Hopefully, this account of their most notable deeds and reputations will do something to redress the balance in favour of a fuller understanding of who they were and how they did their work at the scaffold and the death cell.

Maybe one of the most telling details about these men's beliefs and value systems is a little note in the archives with Steve Wade's materials collected: this is a letter from Winston Churchill, thanking Wade for a birthday contribution. Maybe Wade kept that for reasons of a slight contact with a very famous person, but there is a string implication that here was a symbol of everything the 'true born Englishmen' admired. The 'British bulldog' meant doing chores and undergoing ordeals for one's country, even work of the most distasteful nature.

In the end, one of the most lucid and honest apologias for the hangman's art has been given by Albert Pierrepoint, probably now one of Bradford's most notorious figures from history. Albert wrote:

> During my twenty-five years as an executioner, I believed with all my heart that I was carrying out a public duty. I conducted each execution with great care and a clear conscience. I never allowed myself to get involved with the death penalty controversy.

But this most famous and professionally impressive Yorkshire hangman confessed that beneath the exterior he was, of course, a human being with all the usual emotions and also that his years in that work had persuaded him that it was of no use: 'If death were a deterrent, I might be expected to know. It is I who have faced them last, young lads and girls, working men, grandmothers. I have been amazed by the courage with which they take that walk into the unknown ... All the men and women whom I have faced at that final moment convince me that in what I have done I have not prevented a single murder.'

In the end, the subject of hangmen and hanging will always have that quality of fascination, sometimes morbid but also sometimes simply an example of why and how the human mind needs to know everything, to be curious about all the things people do.

In the Middle Ages, trades were known as 'mysteries' and that implied that the work and lifestyles of people in their trades was something exempt from general knowledge. The story of Yorkshire's hangmen illustrates that gradual dissolution of that 'mystery' which began with mere amateurs learning 'on the job' and ended with celebrity figures who were almost bullied into revealing all. From the historian's point of view, however, there are so many dark corners in the records of crime that there are still plenty of stories to tell and retell.

Selected Bibliography

There is much scattered and piecemeal journalism associated with the literature of hanging. Such sources as chapbooks, ballads and street literature have played their part in making this ephemeral bank of sources for the crime historian. Some of the standard volumes here give collections of such tales in more permanent form. Notable in this respect are the reprints of material from older magazines. I have included only a small number of these, as the source material was slender. But the major works on the history of hanging contain 'leads' to these materials, principally the books by Linebaugh and Bland.

Main Sources

Dernley, Syd, with Newman, David, *The Hangman's Tale* (Hale, London), 1989.

Ellis, John, *Diary of a Hangman* (True Crime Library, London), 1997.

Forshaw (ed.), *Yorkshire Notes and Queries* (Baines, Bradford), 1880.

Furniss, Harold (ed.), *Famous Crimes: Police Budget Edition* (Furniss, London), 1910.

Hawkins, Henry, *Reminiscences of Sir Henry Hawkins* (Nelson, London), 1909.

Pierrepoint, Albert, *Executioner: Pierrepoint* (Hodder and Stoughton), 1974.

Strahan J A, *The Bench and Bar of England*, (Blackwood, Edinburgh and London), 1919.

Watson, Robert Patrick, *A Journalist's Experiences of Mixed Society* (Macmillan, London), 1880.

Punch in Wig and Gown (Educational Book Co., London), 1910.

Steve Wade MSS. In Doncaster Archives: DZ MZ 65/1, letter from Churchill and notes on several cases including the Richter material.

Secondary Sources

Books

Abbott, Geoffrey, *William Calcraft, Executioner Extra-ordinaire* (Eric Dobby: Barming), 2004.

Abbott, Geoffrey, *Execution: A Guide to the Ultimate Penalty* (Summersdale, London), 2005.

Bentley, David, *The Sheffield Murders 1865–1965* (ALD Design and Print, Sheffield), 2003.

Birkenhead, Earl of, *Famous Trials* (Hutchinson, London), 1930.

Bland, James, *The Common Hangman: English and Scottish hangmen before the Abolition of Public Executions* (Zeon, London), 2001.

Davies, Owen, *Murder, Magic, Madness* (Pearson, Harlow), 2005.

Diamond, Michael, *Victorian Sensation: the spectacular, the shocking and the scandalous in nineteenth century Britain* (Anthem press, London), 2003.

Donaldson, William, *Rogues, Villains and Eccentrics* (Phoenix, London), 2002.

Chapman, Pauline, *Madame Tussaud's Chamber of Horrors* (Grafton, London), 1986.

Duff, Charles, *A Handbook on Hanging* [1928 First edition] (Tempus, Stroud), 2006.

Cyriax, Oliver, *The Penguin Encyclopaedia of Crime* (Penguin, London), 1993.

Evans, Stewart P, *Executioner: The Chronicles of James Berry, Victorian Hangman* (Sutton, Stroud), 2004.

Fielding, Steve, *Pierrepoint: A Family of Executioners* (London, Blake), 2006.

Gattrell, V A C, *The Hanging Tree: Execution and the English People 1770–1868*, (OUP, Oxford), 1994.

Goodman, Jonathan, *The Daily Telegraph Murder File*, (Mandarin, London), 1993.

Hibbert, Christopher, *The Roots of Evil: A Social History of Crime and Punishment* (Sutton, Stroud), 2003.

Jackson, Robert, *The Chief: The Biography of Gordon Hewart, Lord Chief Justice of England, 1922-40* (Harrap, London), 1959

Jones, Steve, *Yorkshire: The Sinister Side, Book 1, 1850–80* (Wicked, Nottingham), 2004.

Kadri, Sadakat, *The Trial: A history from Socrates to O J Simpson* (Harper, London), 2006.

Kennedy, Ludovic, *10, Rillington Place* (Gollancz, London), 1961.

Laurence, John, *A History of Capital Punishment* (Sampson, Low and Marston), 1940.

Leech, T J, *A Date with the Hangman* (True Crime Library, London), 1998.

Leonora, Klein, *A Very English Hangman: The Life and Times of Albert Pierrepoint* (Corvo, London), 2006.

Linebaugh, Peter, *The London Hanged*, (Verso, London), 2003.

Lyons, Lewis, *The History of Punishment* (Amber Books, London), 2003.

McLynn, Frank, *Crime and Punishment in 18th century England* (Routledge, London), 1989.

Marjoribanks, Edward, *Famous Trials of Marshall Hall* (Penguin, London), 1950.

Rede, Thomas Leman, *York Castle* (J Saunders, York), 1829.

Scott, George Riley, *The History of Corporal Punishment* (Torchstream, London), 1938.

Thomas, Donald, *The Victorian Underworld*, (John Murray, London), 1998.

Wilkinson, George Theodore, *The Newgate Calendar* [First edition 1828] (Sphere Books, London), 1991.

Periodicals and Reports

Douglas, Robert, 'The Hangman Lights a Cigarette . . .', *The Mail on Sunday*, 29 May 2005.
'Pierrepoint the Hangman Faced the Axe', *Daily Express*, 1 June 2006.
Robin, Gerald D, 'The Executioner: His Place in English Society' in *British Journal of Sociology*, Vol. 15 No. 3 (1964), pp. 234-3.
Illustrated London News.
Journal of the Police History Society.
Lincolnshire Gazette.
Murder Most Foul.
Punch.
The Times Digital Archive.
True Crime.
True Detective.
The Death Penalty in European Countries (Council of Europe, 1962).
Courts of Criminal Appeal (annual).

Web Sites

Back to Billington families in Lancs: www.users.bigpond.com/telglen
York Castle Prisons: www.richard.clark32.btinternet.co.uk/york
The British Female Hanged: www.richard.clark32.btinternet.co.uk/york
Williams, Paul R, *The Ultimate Price: The Unlawful Killing of English Police Officers*: www.murderfiles.com

TRUE CRIME FROM WHARNCLIFFE

Foul Deeds and Suspicious Deaths Series

Barking, Dagenham & Chadwell Heath
Barnsley
Bath
Bedford
Birmingham
Black Country
Blackburn and Hyndburn
Bolton
Bradford
Brighton
Bristol
Cambridge
Carlisle
Chesterfield
Colchester
Coventry
Croydon
Derby
Dublin
Durham
Ealing
Folkestone and Dover
Grimsby
Guernsey
Guildford
Halifax
Hampstead, Holborn and St Pancras
Huddersfield
Hull

Leeds
Leicester
Lewisham and Deptford
Liverpool
London's East End
London's West End
Manchester
Mansfield
More Foul Deeds Birmingham
More Foul Deeds Chesterfield
More Foul Deeds Wakefield
Newcastle
Newport
Norfolk
Northampton
Nottingham
Oxfordshire
Pontefract and Castleford
Portsmouth
Rotherham
Scunthorpe
Southend-on-Sea
Staffordshire and The Potteries
Stratford and South Warwickshire
Tees
Warwickshire
Wigan
York

OTHER TRUE CRIME BOOKS FROM WHARNCLIFFE

A-Z of Yorkshire Murder
Black Barnsley
Brighton Crime and Vice 1800-2000
Durham Executions
Essex Murders
Executions & Hangings in Newcastle
  and Morpeth
Norfolk Mayhem and Murder

Norwich Murders
Strangeways Hanged
The A-Z of London Murders
Unsolved Murders in Victorian and
  Edwardian London
Unsolved Norfolk Murders
Unsolved Yorkshire Murders
Yorkshire's Murderous Women

Please contact us via any of the methods below for more information or a catalogue.

WHARNCLIFFE BOOKS

47 Church Street – Barnsley – South Yorkshire – S70 2AS
Tel: 01226 734555 – 734222 Fax: 01226 – 734438
E-mail: enquiries@pen-and-sword.co.uk
Website: www.wharncliffebooks.co.uk

Index

People

Abbot, Geoffrey 11
Allen, Harry 126, 138–40, 150
Allen, Peter 32
Archer, Alfred 48
Armstrong, George 117
Askern, Thomas 19, 23, 44–5, 149
Atkinson, Matthew 44
Austwick, Constable 56
Avory, Mr Justice 98

Baldwin, Elizabeth 83
Ball, Charlotte 139
Barker, Dudley 80
Barratt, Percy 97
Batty, Charles 43
Baxter, Robert 95
Benson, Benjamin 97
Benson, D 46
Bentley, David 124
Bentley, Derek 102
Berry, James 6, 9, 52, 53–64, 145, 153, 156
Billington, James 65–73
Billington, John 87
Billington, William 72–5, 80
Binns, Bartholomew 20, 47–8, 49, 101
Blake, David 104
Bramley, Tom 127
Brougham, Alfred 137
Bryant, Charlotte 92
Burke, Thomas 47
Burn, Robert 17

Calcraft, William 6, 7, 148, 151, 153
Cardwell, George 97
Cavendish, Lord Frederick 47–8

Christie, John 102, 112
Churchill, Winston 109, 118, 157
Clarkson, James 80–1
Coates, James 42
Connor, James 149
Cooper, William 117
Coulson, John 89
Cream, Neil 68–9
Crosby, Nicholas 135
Curry, William 7, 19, 36–44

Delasalle, Sidney 106–7
Dernley, Syd 9, 133, 134–6
Dickens, Charles 7
Distleman, Harry 105
Dobson, William 43
Dougal, Samuel 72
Douglas, Robert 139, 150
Dove, William 44
Drucke, Karl 105
Drummond, Edward 31
Duff, Charles 115, 144
Dutton, Henry 20

Edwards, William 104–5
Eldon, Lord 29
Ellis, Gregory 86
Ellis, John 79, 92, 133, 143
Ellis, Ruth 32, 102, 155
Ellis, Sarah 80
Ellwood, John 86–7
Elsam, Eleanor 10
Elst, Violet van der 11
Evans, Gwynne 32
Evans, Stewart 54, 56
Evans, Timothy 102

Fairbank, George 10
Farrell, Maureen 128
Faskally, Dr 58

Places